REDISCOVERING
CHRISTIANITY

Other Works by Page Smith

James Wilson: Founding Father

John Adams

The Historian and History

As a City Upon a Hill: A Town in American History

Daughters of the Promised Land: Women in American History

Jefferson: A Revealing Biography

Dissenting Opinions
A People's History of the United States
    (8 volumes)

The Constitution: A Documentary and Narrative History

Killing the Spirit: Higher Education in America

REDISCOVERING CHRISTIANITY

A HISTORY OF MODERN DEMOCRACY AND THE CHRISTIAN ETHIC

BY
PAGE SMITH

ST. MARTIN'S PRESS   NEW YORK

Design by Basha Zapatka

Library of Congress Cataloging-in-Publication Data

Smith, Page.
    Rediscovering Christianity : A history of modern
Democracy and the Christian ethic / Page Smith.
        p.   cm.
    Includes index.
    ISBN 0-312-10531-2
    1. Church and the world.   2. Church and state—United States.
3. Christianity—United States—21st century.   4. Capitalism—
Religious aspects—Christianity.   5. Christianity and politics.
I. Title.
BR115.W6S53   1994
277.3—dc20   93-35894
                                                        CIP

First Edition: January 1994

10 9 8 7 6 5 4 3 2 1

For Freya

CONTENTS

PROLOGUE: THE PROPOSITION   1

1. THE BEGINNING   9

2. THE CHURCH UNIVERSAL   25

3. THE REFORMERS   37

4. COMMUNITIES OF THE LORD   61

5. THE GREAT REBELLION   73

6. THE ENLIGHTENMENT   95

7. DECLARATION AND CONSTITUTION   109

8. RADICAL PROTESTANTISM IN NINETEENTH-CENTURY AMERICA   131

9. POPULISTS AND SOCIALISTS   149

10. THE NEW DEAL   175

EPILOGUE: THE SOLUTION   189

INDEX   201

ABOUT THE AUTHOR   211

REDISCOVERING
CHRISTIANITY

PROLOGUE

THE PROPOSITION

With the end of the Cold War, and the so-called triumph of capitalism, we are left with a number of misconceptions that seriously compromise our ability to think creatively about the future. Americans have always been in a large measure "future-oriented." Our notions about the future have often been naive or simplistic—such as the belief that our children would "do better" than we had done; that the general conditions of life in the United States would be better for everyone; that there would be, inevitably, progress, however defined. We have believed in what Herbert Croly, in the early years of this century, called "the promise of American life," in a best-selling book by that title. America was, in the title of another best-seller by Mary Antin, "the promised land."

Now a strange paralysis has seized us. The malaise began several decades ago and has intensified in the 1990s. We appear to be unable to think about the future. A kind of fatalism has settled on the land. A widely discussed essay, and now a book, is called *The End of History*.

So the next obvious question is, Why is it essential to be able to think about the future? The answer is that the future is shaped by our faith in it. We believe the future into existence. It is shaped by our vision of what it should be; without that vision, the Scriptures tell us, a people perish, a society slips into a kind of hell of selfishness and self-indulgence, where the center does not hold and all is decadence and disintegration.

Traditional utopianism appears dead and I, for one, am not inclined to mourn its passing, but its demise does not relieve us of the obligation of trying to imagine a better future for humankind. The future is inevitably the product of our dreams, however imperfectly realized. It is clearly not the consequence of some "process," although one often sees in it a kind of dialectic. History does not progress inevitably "on and up"; it can very well, and often has, progressed "along and down," and indeed its natural tendency appears to be *down* when there are not enough faithful hearts to sustain it.

I believe that the principal reason for this poverty of the imagination at this moment is that Christianity, which overcame the classical Greek and Roman notion of time as endlessly cyclical by positing a beginning of history and an end, has come to be equated with capitalism. Democracy, as a universal ideal, is also a creation of Christian doctrine, which has always believed in a world where all men and women were equal in the eyes of God and, ultimately, in the world.

Thus Christianity, until the advent of the Enlightenment, of Darwinism, and, finally, of Marxism, was the herald of a future of infinite growth and possibility, an "open" future instead of one of eternal repetition. It seems to me that the principal reason we are presently unable to think about the future, unable to try to think the future into existence, is that—with the collapse of Marxism and Communism—we have bestowed upon capitalism a degree of legitimacy that it has never enjoyed before. Many of us feel in our bones that there must be some more gracious and humane form of economic and political organization than capitalism, something *beyond capitalism*. I believe that the first step in beginning to think about this "beyond" is to disentangle Christianity—and democracy—from capitalism, and to demonstrate that Christianity has been from its inception a tireless critic of, and indeed, the opponent of, those forms of economic activity that we have come to denominate "capitalistic."

This task is admittedly complicated both by our moral and intellectual confusion following the end of the Cold War and by the residual memory of a famous essay by the German sociologist Max Weber. Early in this century, Weber published a work entitled *The Protestant Ethic and the Spirit of Capitalism*. In it, he argued that Protestantism created the "moral climate of opinion" in which modern capitalism was formed and because of which it flourished. Weber was at least a semi-Marxist, and he doubtlessly hoped to kill two birds that enjoyed the disapprobation of Marxism—capitalism and Christianity—with one stone.

In advancing his argument, Weber opened up the kind of controversy that the scholarly world dotes on. For fifty or more years, scholars of various political persuasions and different nationalities amplified, refuted, amended, or extended Weber's argument, which came, essentially, to this: the "Protestant Ethic" of thrift, piety, and hard work resulted in modern capitalism. Thrift encouraged capital accumulation, and hard work resulted in the creation of wealth that could be converted into capital.

While capitalistic ventures have been going on for millennia, modern, post-Reformation capitalism, according to Weber, is distinguished by the "rational . . . organization of [formally] free labour." The development of modern capitalism depended on "the ability and disposition of men to adopt certain types of practical rational conduct. When these types have been obstructed by spiritual obstacles, the development of rational economic conduct has also met serious inner resistance."

The "spiritual obstacles" that Weber refers to as impeding the development of "rational economic conduct" are not, as one might suppose, Protestantism's warnings about wealth and worldliness, but the Roman Catholic Church's injunctions against "usury," which, it is clear, were more honored in the breach than the observance. These injunctions, Weber contends, inhibited the development of "modern capitalism" in fifteenth- and sixteenth-century Europe. The Reformation, on the other hand, relaxed the constraints on "interest," that is on usury, thereby encouraging capital formation and, presumably, "rational economic behavior." In addition, the Reformation stimulated the growth of capitalism by its strong emphasis on the "work ethic."

One interesting thing about the scholars who have for almost a hundred years debated the Weber hypothesis about the influence of Puritanism on the "rise of capitalism" is that even those who have been most critical of the Weber thesis have, without exception so far as I know, conceded that after, let us say, the late seventeenth or early eighteenth century, Puritanism capitulated to capitalism and, indeed, became its enthusiastic advocate and coadjutor. As far as America is concerned, this notion is, as we shall see, in error.

It is a main purpose of this work to demonstrate what should never have been in question, namely, that Christianity has always been resistant to capitalism, to the "spirit of capitalism," to capitalism in whatever form it presented itself. This is not, of course, to say that "the Church" or churches have not often compromised with capitalism and, on occasion, embraced it, but such accommodations were always contrary to Christian doctrine. Much the same could be said for the relationship of capitalism to democracy. Democracy grew without reference to capitalism and often in direct opposition to it. In the nineteenth century, capitalism did its best to subvert democracy by systematically robbing working men and women of the fruits of their labor and using the most ruthless methods of suppression to keep workers in subjection.

It is simply to say that if we are to think clearly about our future, we must know our past. It is not so much that the past has "lessons," although it certainly has, but that it is important to situate ourselves in time. When we begin to get a sense of all that the human race has accomplished and endured, it vastly expands our sensibilities. It gives us a home in time and hope and, I believe, a kind of poise or assurance. Most surprisingly, it gives us *joy*. Why joy? I would say that the dazzling sense of possibilities that history opens up to us through the biographies of our predecessors, which is what history most essentially is, produces a feeling of exhilaration. Delight. Joy. Leopold von Ranke, the nineteenth-century "father" of modern historiography, wrote that joy—the joy one derives from "looking at flowers"—was the gift of history to the historian and, by extension, to his or her readers. It is a bit startling to encounter such testimony from the man considered the prototype of the Germanic historian!

I think it is demonstrable that all thinking and all action are compromised by ignorance of what has gone before. Numerous cultures have survived for centuries and, indeed, millennia without "histories" in the modern (or perhaps better, the eighteenth- and nineteenth-century) sense of that word. They lived, for the most part, in a kind of timeless innocence.

For better or worse, they have been drawn, or propelled, into history. Since we are all now in the same global boat (or inhabitants of the same "global village"), it is essential for us to get our history right. If in the matter before us—the relationship of Christianity to capitalism—we don't get it right, it is hard to see how we can work effectively for the unity of humankind. If we do not comprehend the genesis of the dominant ideas of the modern world, we are condemned to flounder about in a state of increasing moral and intellectual disarray.

The intention of *Rediscovering Christianity* is to trace the genealogy of what I—and, I assume, a great many others—believe to be the guiding principles of our age: (1) democracy, (2) equality before the law, (3) the unity of the peoples of the world (*e pluribus unum*).

It think it can be safely assumed that critics will not be behindhand in disputing my genealogy and offering alternative interpretations of the origins and growth of the "social determinants" that I have enumerated. I believe that whatever discussions may follow, they can only serve to clarify the nature and origin of those principles that have been our guides in the past and must continue to be so if we are to have a humane future.

1

THE BEGINNING

If we are to trace the history of Christian attitudes toward wealth and worldliness, the obvious starting point is the Old Testament. In Christ's teaching on compassion for the "poor and needy," he drew from the rich literature of the Israelites, from the tradition of his own people. Throughout the various books that make up the Old Testament runs a constant refrain of Jehovah's special concern for the "poor and needy." The people of Israel had, after all, been slaves, and severely oppressed slaves, in Egypt. That was the deepest memory of the tribes. This experience tempered all they thought and did, all that their priests and prophets and lawmakers wrote. The references to the "poor and the needy" begin with Exodus (King James translation) (22:25), where God warns against usury: "If thou lend money to any of my people that is poor by thee, thou shalt not be to him as a usurer. . . . "

Mention of the "poor and needy" is, not surprisingly, concentrated in the Books of the Law, specifically Lev-

iticus and Deuteronomy, and in the Psalms of David, the
Proverbs of Solomon, and in Ecclesiastes. They are also
included in the so-called Wisdom Books, containing precepts for living a life favorable in the eyes of the Lord.
In Leviticus, the Hebrews are instructed: ". . . . you shall
not leave your vineyard bare, neither shall you gather the
fallen grapes of your vineyard, you shall leave them for
the poor and the stranger." (23:22 and 25:35)

"And the stranger" is a significant phrase. The Hebrews were a tribal people whose first requirement was
to provide for the members of the tribe, but beyond that,
the tribes were enjoined to "neither vex a stranger nor
oppress him: for ye were strangers in the land of Egypt."

Again, in Leviticus (25:35): "And if thy brother be
waxen poor, and fallen in decay with thee; then thou
shalt relieve him: *yea, though he be* a stranger, or a
sojourner."

In Deuteronomy, it was specified that every seventh
year be proclaimed the year of the "Lord's release," at
which time creditors were enjoined to cancel their loans
to fellow Israelites. "For the poor shall never cease out
of the land and therefore I command thee, saying, Thou
shalt open thy hand wide unto thy brother, to the poor,
and to the needy in thy land."

In addition to the Old Testament's constant emphasis
on the poor and needy, the work abounds with warnings
and admonitions to the rich and powerful. In 1 Samuel
it states: "The Lord . . . raiseth up the poor out of the

dust *and* lifteth up the beggar from the dunghill to set *them* among princes, and to make them inherit the throne of glory. . . . '' (2:8)

Job, in his dramatic dialogue with the Lord, puts great stress on his obedience to the Lord in regard to the poor. He reminds the Lord that he "delivered the poor that cried, and the fatherless. . . . I was a father to the poor," and "Was not my soul grieved for the poor." (29:12–16, 30:25)

In the Psalms, David inveighs against the wicked: "In the secret places doth he murder the innocent: his eyes are privily set against the poor." Conversely: "Blessed is he that considereth the poor: the Lord will deliver him in time of trouble. . . . For he shall stand at the right hand of the poor. . . . ''(41:1, 109:31)

Proverbs, attributed to Solomon, are full of warnings to the proud and powerful: the man "that maketh himself rich, yet *hath* nothing: *there is* [he] that maketh himself poor yet *hath* great riches." "He that oppresseth the poor reproacheth his Maker; but he that honoureth him hath mercy on the poor." "Better is the poor that walketh in his righteousness, than he that is perverse in *his* ways, though he *be* rich." (13:7, 14:31, 28:6) "He who oppresses the poor insults his maker, and he who is kind to the needy honors him. . . . He who closes his ears to the cry of the poor will himself also cry and not be heard." (14:31, 17:5, 21:13, also 19:17)

Ecclesiastes, which is so concerned with the vanities

of the world, is, of all the books of the Bible, the most severe on the rich. The Book begins by reminding us that "the profit of the earth is for all: the king *himself* is served by the field." (5:9): "He that loveth silver shall not be satisfied with silver: nor he that loveth abundance with increase: this *is* also vanity. . . . The sleep of the laboring man is sweet: but the abundance of the rich man will not suffer him to sleep. . . . He who loves money will not be satisfied with money: nor he who loves wealth with gain. . . . "

Isaiah, who anticipates the coming of "the suffering one," declares that "The meek also shall increase *their* joy in the Lord, and the poor among men shall rejoice in the Holy One of Israel."

This sampling of the more than 175 references in the Old Testament to the "poor and needy" should make manifest the depth of the tradition that Christ had to draw on. What he did, in effect, was to universalize these messages.

The essential preoccupation of the Hebrews, as a tribal people, was with justice and compassion for the members of the tribe, or tribes, although, as we have seen, this compassion was extended to "strangers" and "sojourners," men and women who happened to live with or nearby them. The followers of Christ believed that he came to bring this message to the world for its redemption. But even here, of course, there were Biblical antecedents, hints that there had been unity in the world, "And the whole world was of one language" (Gen 11:1), before disobedience brought punishment in the form of the "confusion of tongues." Christ warned in Mark that the truth of the word of salvation would often be compromised by "the cares of this world, and the deceitfulness of riches." (Mark 4:19) "For what is a man profited if he shall gain the whole world, and lose his own soul."

Luke tells us that after Satan tempted Christ, Christ returned to Nazareth, "where he had been brought up," and spoke in the synagogue on the Sabbath, telling the congregation that he had been sent to preach the gospel to the poor . . . to heal the brokenhearted, to preach deliverance to the captives, and the recovering of sight to the blind, to set at liberty them that are bruised.

In Luke 12, Jesus spoke to "an innumerable multitude of people," telling them the parable of "a certain rich man" who sought to acquire such worldly goods as would allow him to take his "ease, eat, drink and be merry." "But God said unto him, Thou fool, this night thy soul shall be required of thee; then whose shall these things be, which thou has provided? So is he that layeth up treasure himself, as is not rich toward God." Then Christ said to his disciples: "Take no thought for your life what ye shall eat; neither for the body what ye shall put on. The life is more than meat, and the body *is more* than rainment."

Then, in some of the most famous words of the New Testament, Christ assured his disciples that, as the Lord provided for the ravens that neither sowed nor reaped and the lilies that "toil not, spin not," and yet are arrayed more brilliantly than "Solomon in all his glory," so would he provide for them. "Sell that ye have, and give alms. . . . " Lay up your treasure in heaven, not on earth, "for where your treasure is, there will your heart be also."

Then there is the famous quotation from Mark: "It is easier for a camel to go through the eye of a needle than for a rich man to enter into the kingdom of God." (Mark 10:25)

It was indeed the same day that a young man came to Jesus and asked what was necessary "that I may inherit eternal life?" Jesus reminded him of the ten commandments. Those he observed faithfully, the young man said. Then Jesus, "beholding him, loved him" and said: "One thing thou lackest; go thy way, sell whatever thou hast, and give to the poor, and thou shall have treasure in heaven; and come, take up the cross and follow me."

We all know, or should know, the young man's response: "He was sad at that saying, and went away grieved; for he had great possessions."

Such verses could be multiplied many times over. Those quoted above will simply remind us that the overriding theme of the New Testament is the superiority of the spiritual life to the material, the life of the world.

Another primary theme in the New Testament is the relation of Christianity to the world. Jesus constantly reminded his disciples that the gospel is to be preached not to this group or that, but to the *whole world*. He hoped to impart to them an aspiration to reach out to every nation, to every people, and unite them in one universal Christian community, wherein to lay the seeds of democracy and equality.

We know something of the struggles of the early Christian communities from the letters of St. Paul, of James, and of Peter, to the various congregations of the faithful. That they were poor and persecuted we know, and that they experienced the trials and temptations of the world is evident enough. St. Paul writes to Timothy, who has complained about the austerity of life in his community: "Having food and rainment, let us be therewith content. For the love of money is the root of all evil." (6:10)

That these early communities were the prototype of Christian democracy and equality we know also.

Christian doctrine stressed the fact that the faithful held a kind of duel citizenship; they were members of the community of believers, but they were also citizens of the world—"Be ye in the world but not of it," Christians were told.

Matthew, Mark, and Luke all tell of Jesus's response to the Pharisees when they tried to trap him into denying it was proper for one of his followers to pay taxes to Caesar. Jesus's answer is one of the most familiar in the New Testament: " 'Why tempt me, ye hypocrites? Show me the tribute money.' And they brought unto him a penny. And he saith unto them, 'Whose is this image and superscription?' And they said unto him, 'Caesar's.' Then he saith unto them: 'Render to Caesar the things which are Caesar's: and to God the things that are God's.' "

That famous exchange laid the foundation for the relationship in Christendom between the Church and the State in all their subsequent forms for at least the next two thousand years. It made it unnecessary, as well as unwise, for the Christian community to confront the Roman state. It established the fact that, however intimate the relationship between Church and the State might at times be, they were indeed two identifiably different spheres.

From a few thousand beleaguered men and women, Christianity grew. It was especially appealing, of course, to the more marginal members of the Roman Empire, but it also in time attracted many members of the upper classes. In 306 A.D., the man who came to be known as Constantine the Great was recognized by his troops as the head of the Roman Empire. Six years later, in the course of defeating an insurgent general, Constantine saw in the sky a cross with the Latin words *in hoc signo vinces*: "in this sign victory." Not long afterward, he became a Christian, and in the Edict of Milan he proclaimed the freedom of all religions. While other religions were free to expound their doctrines, Christianity became the official religion of the Empire. It was an unexpected triumph for a faith that had been persecuted for some three hundred years.

The Christian Church, gaining power through the favor of Constantine and his successors, flourished and grew rich and powerful in the process. That story, fascinating in itself, lies beyond the scope of this work.

Suffice it to say that a process of centralization took place. Bishops, who were originally "overseers," gained power at the cost of the individual congregations. The bishops of the large and richer "sees" not surprisingly gained the most power. They came to be called "metropolitans." Five "patriarchs" presided over the churches of Rome, Jerusalem, Antioch, Alexandria, and Constantinople.

The Eastern churches went very much their own way, while in the West, the Bishop of Rome gained precedence over his peers, being acknowledged as holding the "presidency in charity." While the Latin Fathers of the Church—Ambrose, Jerome, Eusebius among them—expounded Christian doctrine with great skill and subtlety (Max Weber declared that "the full development of a systematic theology must be credited to Christianity"), the Roman Empire disintegrated. Its collapse was an event so extraordinary, literally so incomprehensible, that even its enemies were incredulous. St. Jerome wrote on hearing the news: "A terrible rumor reaches me from the West, telling of Rome besieged, bought for gold, besieged again, life and property perishing together. My voice falters, sobs stifle the words I dictate; for she is captive, that city which enthralled the world."

It was at this moment that Augustine, Bishop of Hippo, began his great treatise, *The City of God*. Augustine took as his text Christ's reply to the Pharisee: "Render to Caesar the things that are Caeser's, and to God the things that are God's." (Mark 12:17)

At the prompting of his friend Marcellinus, who had been sent to North Africa by the Emperor Honorius to resolve a dispute, Augustine began to make his case for the truth of Christianity over other creeds. Marcellinus, in the course of his mission, had become a friend of the proconsul of Africa, an unusually intelligent and able man named Volusian. Although a pagan, Volusian was drawn strongly to Christianity. His principal problem was that he found it difficult to reconcile the life of a Christian with his obligations as an official of the Roman Empire, so it was to this problem specifically that Marcellinus urged Augustine to address his arguments.

In the course of doing so, Augustine turned his work into a kind of *omnium gatherum* of reflections and asides on virtually every aspect of Christian life and doctrine. It can also be read as a kind of resumé of the writings of earlier Fathers of the Church, such as Tertullian and Justin. Begun in 413 A.D. and finished thirteen years later, *The City of God* occupied Augustine from the age of fifty-nine to seventy-two and thus may be taken as the fruit of his most mature thought and reflection.

Augustine was rankled by the fact that many non-Christians blamed the collapse of the Roman Empire on the elevation of Christianity to its official religion. This act of Constantine, they declared, so offended the old Roman gods that they brought the empire down in ruins. "It was this," Augustine wrote, "which kindled my zeal for the house of God, and prompted me to undertake the defense of the city of God against the charges and misrepresentations of its assailants.'' His first ten books were devoted primarily to refuting those pagan charges; the second twelve were devoted to what might be called ''affirmative'' arguments. The first four books of the second section contain Augustine's account ''of the origin of these two cities—the city of God, and the city of the world.'' The next four tell of the ''history or progress'' of the cities and the final four of their ''deserved destinies.''

Speaking of the desire of the rulers of the Imperial City for unity, Augustine wrote that Rome ''endeavored to impose on subject nations not only her yoke, but her languages, as a bond of peace, for that interpreters, far from being scarce, are numberless.'' But this unity had been achieved by ''how many great wars, how much slaughter and bloodshed. . . . And though these are past, the end of these miseries has not yet come,'' referring to the last, bitter days of the Roman Empire. ''Of this vast material for misery,'' Augustine added, ''the earth is full, and therefore it is written, 'is not human life upon earth a trial?' In the face of such facts, would it not be prudent for the citizen of the city of God to withdraw from the city of man much in the spirit of the stoics and try to ride out the storm, confident in joys of the hereafter?''

Augustine emphatically rejected such a course. Fallen, dangerous, and corrupt as the city of man was, the true Christian was a citizen of that city as well. His task was to minister to it as best he could while remaining uncontaminated by it. For one thing, he had within him all the corruptions so evident in the city of man itself. He must dwell in both cities; that was the burden of his humanity. But by the same token he could dwell in the city of God during his time on earth with the heavenly joy that he could anticipate in the life beyond. In the present and the future world, now and in the hope of the world to come, he might rest in his bliss in the bosom of the Lord, acknowledging the Lord as the Master of the Universe and the source of all good. So there it was, two cities, two separate spheres, linked to the end of time, but profoundly different and easily distinguishable, sometimes closer and sometimes further apart. The cities of man, one might say, both against and dependent upon the enduring city of God; the cities of man rising and falling, living and dying, the city of God having the perpetual hope of redemption through the eternal city. It was not Rome that was the eternal city. Despite all its power and glory, it had gone down to humiliation and ruin at the hands of barbarians. If Rome was to live again, it would live as the reborn offspring of the true eternal city.

Again and again, Augustine stresses that ''the things necessary for this mortal life are used by both kinds of men and families alike, but each has its own peculiar and widely different aim in using them. The earthly city, which does not live by faith, seeks an earthly peace, and the end it proposes, in the well-ordered concord of civic obedience and rule, is the combination of men's wills to attain the things which are helpful to this life. The heavenly city, or rather that part of it which sojourns on earth and lives by faith, makes use of this peace only because it must, until this mortal condition . . . shall pass away.'' Therefore as long as it lives ''like a captive and a stranger in the earthly city, though it has already received the promise of redemption, and the gift of the Spirit as the earnest of it, it makes no scruple to obey the laws of the earthly city, whereby the things necessary for the maintenance of this mortal life are administered; and thus, as this life is common to both cities, so there is a harmony between them in regard to what belongs to it.''

On the other hand, it was clear enough that ''the two cities could not have common laws of religion,'' and that in all such matters the city of God must affirm its faith. There still remained, however, a wide field for mutual ventures aimed at the public good. The city of God, for example, can speak in its ''universal voice.'' While it ''sojourns on earth,'' the heavenly city can call ''citizens out of all nations, and [gather] together a society of pilgrims of all languages, not scrupling about diversities in the manners, laws, and institutions whereby earthly peace is secured and maintained, but recognizing that, however various these are, they all tend to one and the same end of earthly peace.''

It is, in simple fact, the earthly witness of the city of God that has the power to reach beyond the boundaries of the particular cities of man with their bitter rivalries and divisions to adumbrate the larger vision of peace and reconciliation. Thus, the heavenly city, ''while in its state of pilgrimage [to the city beyond death] seeks, in the name of all humanity, peace on earth,'' and, so far as it can ''without injuring faith and godliness, desires and maintains common agreement among men regarding the acquisition of the necessaries of life, and makes this earthly peace bear upon the peace of heaven; for this alone can be truly called and esteemed the peace of the reasonable creatures, consisting as it does in the perfectly ordered and harmonious enjoyment of God and of one another in God . . . for the life of the city is a social life.''

I believe these words of Augustine are a charter, one that has been fulfilled in the process of creating the order of the modern world, as imperfect as that order may be. The original blueprint, so to speak. Here is the doctrine of rendering to Caesar what is Caesar's and to the Lord that which is the Lord's—enunciated by Jesus on the eve of his crucifixion, and brilliantly elaborated by Augustine. The power to speak both for and beyond the city of man was to be found only in the essential and transcendent voice of the city of God. There will always be a power beyond all parochialism, nationalism, tribalism beyond the insistent and untiring pull of clan and race. If we are not constantly called forward to that larger vision of humanity, we fall back into the narrowest and pettiest concerns of self.

Not only was the Christian to dwell in the city of man, the Christian was required to serve it. True piety is to be found in virtue, and virtue is to live for the service of others, one's country, one's family, one's friends and neighbors. It is one's duty to beget children. That cannot be done without pleasure, "for there is pleasure in eating and drinking, pleasure also in sensual intercourse." But it is when these products of a virtuous life are made into its primary objectives, into pleasures in themselves, that life is made "hideous," for "where virtue is made the slave of pleasure it no longer deserves the name of virtue."

Augustine is especially eloquent in describing the trials and tribulations of life in the city of man. In addition to the manifold frailities of the body, grief over the illnesses and deaths of loved ones, the natural dangers and accidents to life on earth, there are more intimate dangers. Augustine quotes Cicero on the "snares . . . which lurk . . . under the name of relationship," specifically, "those inflicted by your family," the most desperate wounds of all: "this hidden, intestine, domestic danger" that "overwhelms you before you can see and examine it." Augustine adds, from Matthew, "A man's foes are those of his own household," "words which one cannot hear without pain. . . . If, then, home, the natural refuge from the ills of life, is itself not safe, what shall we say of the city, which, as it is larger, is so much the more filled with lawsuits civil and criminal, and is never free from fear, if sometimes from the actual outbreak of disturbing and bloody insurrections and civil wars?"

Augustine has a good deal to say about the nature of civil government in the city of man. For Augustine, one measure of a true republic was a simple one. Did it serve the common weal, the well-being of its citizens, and, above all, did it ensure justice? Augustine quoted Cicero's definition of a people: "An assemblage associated by a common acknowledgment of right and by a community of interests . . . most certainly it follows that there is no republic where there is no justice."

What seems to me most illuminating about Augustine's treatment of the two cities—the city of man and the city of God—is his compassionate treatment of the city of man. It is a city that Augustine was thoroughly familiar with. We know from his *Confessions* that he had lived there a good portion of his life. He thus knew its joys and its miseries firsthand.

Since Augustine's *City of God* dealt with the most catastrophic event in modern history, it is not surprising that another catastrophe, coming a thousand years later and, if anything, on an even larger scale, should have drawn the attention of theologians and scholars back to Augustine's great work. In the thirty years that ended the turbulent fifteenth century, twenty new editions of the *City of God* were published.

2

THE CHURCH UNIVERSAL

The task of the Church after the distintegration of the
Roman Empire was *to hold the world together for a
thousand years and preserve the vision of a common
future for humankind*. It was a formidable undertaking.
From the westernmost shores of Ireland east to Constantinople, from the margins of the North Sea to the sands
of Africa, through a dozen climates and dozens of dis-
parate races and peoples, provinces, kingdoms, fiefdoms,
the Church exerted its unifying impulse. In the parish
churches of England, Scotland, Wales, and Ireland, in the
cathedrals and churches that dotted the European coun-
tryside, in the vast, complex bureaucracy of the Church
establishment, and, perhaps above all, in the monastaries
and convents, the sense of coherent order was preserved.
Among other unifying measures a "universal calendar"
for the Church year was established. Perhaps the most
potent symbol of the Church's order was the designation
of the use of Latin as the language of the Church universal. The liturgies and forumularies of the Church that

were employed in every part of Europe where the Church put down roots bound the medieval world together. Roman law and canon law provided, at least initially, a semblance of justice for lord and peasant alike.

The Bendictines set the pattern for monastic life by designating an abbot as head of each monastery, giving the separate monasteries a large degree of autonomy and establishing procedures for admission to the monastic life. Much emphasis was laid on work, especially agricultural work and labor in the open air. In the words of the *Encyclopedia of World History*, "The order became the chief instrument for the reform of the [Gallic] Church, and for the conversion and civilization of England and Germany." It has been estimated that in addition to numerous popes and cardinals and five thousand saints (which is certainly a good many saints), the Benedictines alone sustained more than fifteen thousand writers and scholars.

Out of the Bendictine order came others, perhaps the most important being the Cistercians, who reformed the Benedictines and founded monasteries in the most inhospitable places of Europe, in the process laying the foundations for modern agriculture. It is, for a fact, hard to overestimate the role of the monasteries in preserving some degree of civility, in creating and protecting art and scholarship, and, above all, in ministering to the spiritual and practical needs of the ordinary men and women on whom feudalism bore most heavily.

The rebellious monastery of Cluny was powerful

enough to challenge Rome. It was the monks of Cluny who invented the *treuga del*, the peace of the land. In the words of the historian Eugene Rosenstock-Huessy, "Holy Week was epoch-making in that it divided life . . . into peace and war, making peace and war definite, abolishing their complete confusion; and ennobling the task of the common knight as the defense of God's peace."

It was also Cluny that gave the Church one of its most significant days—All Souls. Coming in November, the day after All Saints, which celebrates the triumph of the faithful, All Souls' Day "established the solidarity of all souls from the beginning of the world to the end of time." It was thus the most powerful expression of Christian democracy, of the idea that all souls could be reconciled in God, the Ruler of the Universe, and in his son Jesus Christ. It was thus the ultimate expression of faith in the unity of the race. We are accustomed in this enlightened age to speak quite casually of "one world" or "universal" this or that without any comprehension of the source of such phrases that counter all our instinctive tribal and parochial tendencies.

"So-called world history became a reality," Rosenstock-Huessy wrote, "from the moment when All Souls began to work on every man. . . . All Souls is the cornerstone of . . . our modern civilization."

One of the most important accomplishments of the Medieval Church was to elevate the status of women far beyond that of any other culture. The seeds of this elevation lay in Christ's close relationship to women. The role of women in the world empires that preceded the rise of Christianity was almost uniformly deplorable. Those world empires had solved the problem of the sexual appetites of men by dividing women into two main categories: first as wives and mothers who were not expected to be notably adept as sexual partners (they had other, more important responsibilities, running households and producing and raising children). The second category, which was given official or semiofficial (and even sometimes religious) status, was woman-as-sexual-creature, or, as we would say today, "sex object." Such a division, the early, and later, church set its face against.

Mary Magdalene, a reformed prostitute, was the primary and enduring symbol of the Christian determination to subdue the restless monster of sex, and there were numerous other women among the followers of Jesus. When Jesus dined with the disciples two days before his crucifixion, a woman came and poured a "precious ointment" on his head. The disciples were indignant at this intrusion. The ointment, they protested, should have been sold and the money given to the poor, but Jesus rebuked them, saying that the oil was for his burial. "Verily, I say unto you, wheresoever this gospel shall be preached in the whole world there shall also this, that this woman hath done, be told for a memorial of her."

While the early church preferred the celibate life to a life involving sexual activity (in part, apparently, because the early fathers anticipated the imminent end of the world), Paul declared to the members of the church at

Corinth that it was better to "burn" with sexual desire than to indulge in promiscuous sexual relations. It was, by the same token, better to marry in order to have an outlet for sexual passions than to engage in fornication or adultery (an injunction which was by no means new, having been carried down from Mt. Sinai by Moses at least twice in the form of the seventh commandment).

A classic statement of the attitude of the Church toward women is that of the English cleric John Wyclif, who wrote at the end of the fourteenth century: "When women have been turned fully to goodness, full hard it is that any man pass them in goodness. And as hard it is that any man pass them in sin when they have been turned to pride and lecherie and drunkenness." So it is in every literature: women have been seen by men with profound ambivalence—beings of special grace on the one hand and temptresses on the other. The roots of such attitudes undoubtedly lay in the Church's anxieties about sexual sin and its social consequences.

Modern wise men have pointed to this Christian doctrine as an example of the repressive attitude of the Church toward "healthy, natural, caring" sex relations. What they seldom acknowledge is that by refusing to accept the pagan division of women into wives/mothers on the one hand and sexual playthings on the other, the Church ennobled both women and the institution of marriage itself.

The Medieval Church carried all this considerably further by establishing convents for women who, by choice or necessity, remained single. Nuns were the "Brides of Christ" (surely a high vision of woman's role). Their convents were small islands of peace and security in the disorderly world of the Middle Ages and generation after generation of nuns performed good services for those whom the world neglected or despised. The abbesses who headed the convents were the first, or certainly among the first, female executives, presiding over small domains that stretched far beyond the convent enclosures.

More important still, the Holy Mother, the Virgin Mary, was elevated by the Medieval Church (or by the faithful peasantry) to a position that at times appeared to threaten the eminence of God the Father.

It is enough to say here that the Medieval Church gave women a kind of centrality, and spiritual dignity, not achieved elsewhere. The dominating symbol was the Holy Mother herself, but she was reinforced and supported by a number of women saints. The fact is that the iconography of the Medieval Church demonstrates more powerfully than words the central, if not primary, role of women in the life of the Church.

It might be noted here that a subsidiary of the lives of the monks and nuns who worshiped in monasteries and convents was the ongoing demonstration, most notably in the sexual area, of the reality of faithful lives lived without sex. Since the Church proclaimed the importance of suppressing promiscuity in the name of a higher spiritual life, it was important to exemplify that principle in two of the main institutions of the Church, monasteries and convents.

It was not only in the institutional church that women were elevated to positions of dignity and honor, for the world "outside" was enthralled with the theme of women as superior beings. The tradition of courtly love, celebrated in the poems and songs of the troubadours, idealized women, as in Jean Renart's *Bel Inconnu* (the *Beautiful Unknown*), written in the late twelfth or early thirteenth century. Renart's theme, in the words of one historian, was "that God created woman that man might honor and serve her, woman the source of everything good. The denial of love is blind folly. Woman is endowed by God with everything good and those who speak evil of her fall under God's curse of dumbness."

It is simple enough to test the proposition that Christianity exalted women; the industrious researcher has only to turn up other cultures where the status of women is as high. So far as I am aware no one has yet done so.

The status that women enjoyed through church and convent was reflected in the civic world. In the words of the German historian Friedrich Heer, "The women of Paris are known to have been engaged in more than a hundred different occupations. They worked as weavers, embroiderers, and retailers; when their husbands died they carried on their businesses with resource and courage, proving themselves master craftsmen in their own right; they were teachers, doctors, and merchants."

Once dismissed as the Dark Ages (the period from the Fall of Rome in 400 A.D. to the early years of the so-called Renaissance, circa fourteenth century), historians now understand that the Middle Ages was a period in which many modern forms developed and in which, above all, the idea of a universal human order gained currency with kings and common folk alike.

All institutions, however noble their original purposes and however awesome their accomplishments, become in time rigid, corrupt, and obtuse. This fact is, of course, the principle of original sin writ large in the greater society. Success brings power, and power, sooner or later, corrupts. This was, not surprisingly, the fate of the Medieval Church. Its theological speculations, which once invigorated all thought about human beings and their relation to the mundane and divine (and which laid the foundation for the great universities of Paris, Padua, and Rome and established the foundations for modern scholarship), grew increasingly refined and sterile, remote from the real world and irrelevant to the lives of ordinary people.

In the fifteenth century, with the Church in a state of advanced decay (two rival popes, one worse than the other, contended for the Papal throne), poets, artists, scholars, and intellectuals generally found a new fascination in classical culture, especially, of course, that of fifth-century B.C. Athens. That interest was sparked by an odd and dramatic event. Perplexed by the dilemma of surplus popes, the College of Cardinals settled on an obscure priest named Otto Colonna as a compromise candidate and rushed him through the required steps—bishop, archbishop, cardinal to pope. As Pope Martin V, this obscure prelate set out for Rome (he had been declared pope in 417). It took him three years to get there, and when he arrived, he decided that it would be good policy to invite the Primate of Constantinople and his retinue to Rome to try to reconcile differences between Rome and the Eastern Church.

The arrival in the Holy City of the Eastern contingent caused great excitement and helped to stimulate the newest intellectual fad—Greek thought and culture. The result was what came to be called Christian Humanism, a movement that sought to elevate man, the noblest work of the Almighty. One consequence was the inevitable diminishment of God. An infatuation with things Greek soon became a weapon against the stifling authority of the Church. If one considered the matter to a degree objectively, it was a most curious development. The Greeks had, to be sure, invented abstract thought, "philosophy," as it came to be called, the contemplation of the nature of the material and immaterial world. Greek playwrights had written a substantial number of the greatest plays penned by humankind, Greek sculpture and architecture had attained a perfection that became the wonder and the envy of succeeding generations. But the moment of high Greek, or, more accurately, Athenian culture, was as brief as it was brilliant. It lasted roughly fifty years. It changed nothing in the manner of men's and women's lives. I think it is safe to say that much as it enhanced the artistic and intellectual life of the race, the world would be much the same today without it. The actual lives of the Greeks were as far from the ideal image of, say, Plato's *Republic* (which was, in fact, a rigid dictatorship) as one could well imagine. The history of the Greek city-states is a history, in the main, of continual external wars and internal chaos.

Moreover, the Greeks were an intensely proud and exclusive people, contemptuous of the barbarian (as they put it) cultures around them. What the obsession with Classical, and particularly with Greek, culture meant was that (using St. Augustine's system) the city of man found a religion opposed to that of the city of God. That philosophy represented, to be sure, a substantial misreading of Greek thought. By a process of transmutation, the often wildly irrational Greeks were put forward as the exemplars of rationality, science, and reason.

The humanist scholars thus turned the Christian world on its head. Where the Church had taken God as the measure of all things necessary to the life of a Christian, the new scholars, exhilarated by the prospect of breaking free of the increasingly confining dictates of the Church, proclaimed: "Man is the measure of all things." That sentence was the battle cry of the new learning. The great works of Greek philosophers and natural historians, playwrights, and sculptors were dusted off and elevated to a new canon. The Church, in the great libraries of the Vatican and in the studies of the monks, had preserved the memory of such Greeks as Plato and Aristotle and indeed gave special attention to Aristotle as being closest to Christian thought. For a long time it appeared that the philosophy of Plato and Aristotle might eclipse the teachings of Christ and the doctrines of the Church.

Beginning in the fifteenth century, we have the first serious challenge to the heretofore all-encompassing cosmology of the Christian Church. It appears within the Church itself, gradually assumes the character of an identifiable heresy, and then moves, bag and baggage, from the city of God to the city of man, there to take up permanent residence.

3

THE REFORMERS

Almost a century before the Christian humanists began their romance with ancient Greece, a storm was brewing that would shake Christendom to its foundations and usher in the modern age. In England, a young, Oxford-trained priest began to challenge the whole vast corrupt structure of the papacy. John Wyclif, born in 1320, was a scholar of Balliol College, Oxford, and the university, it might be noted, was a strong ally throughout his career. As an Oxford lecturer, Wyclif attracted a number of students and made a name for himself as an able philosopher. He received several "prebends" or livings from Rome and attained the title of doctor of theology in 1372. Parliament was in one of its periodic states of resistance to the claims of Rome, and had drawn up, perhaps with Wyclif's aid, a bill enumerating fourteen instances of ecclesiastical abuses. Thus it might be said that his original engagement was political rather than theological.

Wyclif believed the line that the world was created by God at a specific time from which it followed that man could produce "nothing except that which God had already created." This formula provided the foundation for the distinctively Protestant doctrines of predestination *and* free will. Stated simply, it is the proposition that God, being all powerful, has foreknowledge of all that is to come. An obvious corollary is that he has known from the beginning of time who was to be saved and who damned. If it were otherwise, that is to say, if human beings by their behavior, by embracing good and abjuring evil, could win salvation, or, conversely, by embracing evil could bring upon themselves eternal damnation, that would represent a diminishment of God's absolute power of which his foreknowledge was an essential part. At the same time, paradoxically, God has given his children free will so that they might behave responsibly in the world.

In the true Christian community, Wyclif argued, all property was held in common for the good of all. Private property was the consequence of sin; it was a symbol of the failure of the community to honor the principles of Christian democracy and equality; it was the serpent in the garden. "In the life of Christ and His gospel," Wyclif wrote,

> that is His testament, with the life and teaching of His apostles [teach not riches] but poverty, meekness . . . travail, and dispising of worldly men for the reproving of their sins. . . . Perforce Jesus Christ was poor in His life. . . . He had no house of His own by worldly title to rest His

head therein, as He Himself says in the gospel. And Saint Peter was so poor that he had neither gold or silver to give a poor crooked man. . . . And Jesus confirming His testament said to His apostles after his rising from death to life, My Father sent me and I send you [to] travail, persecution, and poverty and hunger and martyrdom in this world and not to worldly pomp as clerks [clergy] do now.

The basis for all ecclesiastical authority, Wyclif argued, was righteousness. Thus ecclesiastics and princes of the Church who lived unrighteous lives forfeited their authority and whatever property went with it. Moreover, the Church, Wyclif insisted, was not concerned with temporal matters and it was perfectly legitimate for the civil power to strip the Church of its various properties when the officers of the Church no longer performed the services to which, presumably, they had been called.

Such teachings called into question the whole vast material structure of the Church. Wyclif was summoned to appear before the bishop of London. He came with a retinue of powerful supporters including Lord Percy, one of the most powerful men in England, but before the hearing even began, the advocates of the opposing parties fell to brawling among themselves and a riot ensued.

Under pressure to recant, Wyclif went on the offensive, going so far as to denounce the pope as the Antichrist (this would, before long, become the quasi-official position of reformers in general). Not satisfied with making his propositions the subject of tracts and sermons, Wyclif trained simple itinerate priests to spread his doctrines among the common people. The position of the Roman Church, Wyclif argued, "was that Christ gave the Scriptures to the clergy and doctors of the Church that they might minister sweetly to the laity and to the weaker persons." The fear was that if the Scriptures were translated into the vulgar tongue they might be read by "lewd persons" or misinterpreted and thereby cause mischief. To translate them into the vernacular would mean, in the Church's view, that "the pearl of the gospel is scattered abroad and trodden under foot by swine."

It was Wyclif's conviction that "Christian men and women, old and young, should study . . . in the New Testament, for it is of full authority, and open to understanding of simple men, as to points that most be needful to salvation. . . . Perforce no simple man of wit be afeard unmeasurably to study in the text of Holy Writ, for those be the words of everlasting life. . . . "

It followed that the Bible should be translated so that it could be taught "in the tongue that is more known." For that reason, Wyclif constantly pressed for an English translation to the point where the translation made in his lifetime was credited to him. In his last years, he wrote many of his sermons and essays in English to make them available to those of his compatriots who could not read Latin.

In a time when the poor were looked upon as scarcely

human, Wyclif espoused their cause. In 1381, efforts by landlords to reimpose discarded forms of servile tenure brought a bloody peasant uprising. Manor houses were destroyed, records of tenancy burned, and landlords killed. It has been estimated that some 100,000 peasants made up a ragtag army of desperate men and women. Among the by-no-means unreasonable demands of the peasants was that they be allowed to choose their own pastors, that serfdom be abolished, that the enclosed lands, formerly farmed and now used for pasture, be restored to farming, and that they be given the right to fish and hunt.

Led by Jack Straw and Wat Tyler, the army marched to London, where a number of public officials and lawyers were murdered. John of Gaunt's great mansion was burned, the Tower of London seized, and Archbishop Sudbury, chancellor of England, was murdered. Gulled with false promises, and with their leader, Wat Tyler, killed, the peasant army was finally dispersed after it had threatened to topple the already-rickety structures of English feudalism. Many people blamed Wyclif and his heretical doctrines for stirring up the revolt and he was appealed to condemn the rebels. To his credit, he refused, declaring that the merciless exactions of the great landholders were to blame. A hundred and fifty years later, when the German peasants revolted over many of the same grievances, Martin Luther denounced them and thereby drew a sharp line between the English Reformation and its German counterpart.

Perhaps conscious that he had stretched the patience

of the established order, sympathetic though it might be to those of his teachings that opposed Rome, Wyclif confined his more radical theories to his writings in Latin. But in their persistent bias against property, his works contained the seed of the "leveling" or "communist" doctrines put forward by subsequent reformers.

Wyclif died of a stroke in 1383. More than three decades later, in 1417, the new pope, Martin V, acting on the instructions of the Council of Constance, ordered his body dug up and burned as that of a heretic.

The followers of Wyclif were known as "Lollards." In the period following Wyclif's death, enough Englishmen of substance supported the Lollard cause to give it some credibility, and in 1393, *Twelve Conclusions* drafted by the Lollards were presented to Parliament. Among them were the condemnation of celibacy of the clergy as contributing to "nnatural lust," while vows of chastity by nuns often resulted, the Conclusions declared, in abortions and child murder. Confessions, pilgrimages, special (and expensive) rites for the dead, and the worship of "images" were also condemned.

As time passed, Lollardy became increasingly associated with resistance to the established order and its ranks were made up of the more marginal members of English society. Its followers were hunted down ruthlessly, forced to recant or burned at the stake.

Wyclif's followers and his teachings went so far underground in England that it was several centuries before they reappeared; the first work of Wyclif, published in England, was his *Trialogus*, which appeared in 1525, almost a hundred and fifty years after his death. His writings were carried from England to Europe by a Bohemian monk named Jerome, who translated them into German.

Jerome brought Wyclif's writings to a receptive reader, a young Czech priest of peasant stock named Jan Hus. Hus was born circa 1369 and licensed to preach in the Czech language in 1402. So strong was the influence of Wyclif that his treatises, found in Hus's papers after Hus had been burned at the stake for heresy, were assumed to have been by Hus.

Hus proclaimed the basic propositions that in one form or another would characterize the so-called Reformation. He attacked the Church's sale of indulgences, a scandal whereby the Church *sold* forgiveness to sinners, especially to rich sinners, who were usually the most enterprising. The practice allowed sinners to sin without fear, theoretically at least, of ending in limbo or Hell, and it was a principal business enterprise of the Holy See in its various forms. Hus challenged the authority of the pope. He called for extensive reforms in all levels of the Church hierarchy and, like Wyclif, declared the superior authority of the Scriptures in all issues involving the life of the faithful. He found strong support among the Czech nobility, notably in Queen Sophia, wife of the Emperor Wenceslaus IV. Called to the Council of Constance under a safe-conduct pass, Hus and Jerome were betrayed, arrested, convicted of heresy, and burned at the stake. The Hussite movement gathered strength after Hus's death and became a major element in the subsequent history of Bohemia and Moravia.

The next phase of what would come to be called the Reformation took place in Germany and involved a well-born monk who was teaching at the newly founded university of Wittenberg. On the eve of All Saints Day in 1517, Martin Luther, in one of the most legendary events of modern history, nailed ninety-five Theses to the door of the castle church, thereby setting in motion a movement that would change the course of history. The stage had been set for Luther's ninety-five Theses by the decision of Pope Leo to build the Basilica of St. Peter's. He intended to finance the venture by stepping up the sale of indulgences, already, as we have seen, a sore issue throughout Western Christendom. Luther took advantage of the arrival of a papal agent peddling indulgences to nail his Theses to the door. Not surprisingly, most of the ninety-five Theses had to do with the scandal of indulgences. Number fifty was typical: "Christians should be taught that, if the Pope were acquainted with the exactions of the preachers of pardons, he would prefer that the Basilica of St. Peter's should be burnt to ashes, than it should be built with the skin, flesh and bones of his sheep."

The general tone of the Theses was that the pope himself could not, of course, know of the terrible corruption of those who acted in his name. Luther even wrote a long, unctuous letter to Leo assuring him that his criticisms of Rome were not directed at the pope personally, but rather at the abuses that he was apparently unable to control or correct. The fact was that Luther was as subtle a politician as he was an eloquent expounder of theological doctrine. One of his most important tracts was addressed to the German nobility. In it he played skillfully upon German pride, upon the resentment of the German nobility at the high-handedness of the papal establishment, and on the right of Germany to run its own ecclesiastical affairs without dictation from the pope. The "German nation," he wrote, "the bishops and princes, should remember that they are Christians and should defend the people, who are committed to their government in temporal and spiritual affairs, from these ravenous wolves in sheep's clothing [the functionaries of Rome] that profess to be shepherds and rulers. . . . " He also held out an olive branch to the Hussites, who had often been at odds with the German nobility.

Luther's *Address to the German Nobility* was published three years after his Theses. It was read as avidly by Germans of all classes. Politically motivated as much of it was, its most essential elements were theological. The "Romanists," Luther declared, had built three walls around the papacy to guard it from any effort at reform. The first of these walls was the argument that the temporal authority was subordinate to that spiritual authority that Rome professed to exercise. By this proposition no wickedness or criminal act done by any ecclesiastic from the lowliest friar to the pope himself could be punished by the temporal power, that is to say, the civil courts. In

Luther's words: "Forasmuch as the temporal power has been ordained of God for the punishment of the bad and the protection of the good, therefore we must let it do its duty throughout all the Christian body, without respect of persons, whether it strikes popes, bishops, priests, monks, nuns, or whoever it may be." If the picture of churchly corruption that has come down to us is in any way accurate, the rigorous application of Luther's doctrine would have resulted in half or more of the Church's hierarchy being jailed or suffering even more severe penalties. Luther implied as much, asking, "Why do we leave the greed of Rome so unpunished that it is the greatest thief and robber that has appeared or can appear on earth? . . . "

To place the spiritual authorities above the civil law was to accept the notion that priests and other officers of the Church were of some superior order, ranking higher in the eyes of the Lord than ordinary men and women. The fact was that God had declared all believers to be priests and kings; it was mere chance or election that one among them exercised, in the name of all, certain priestly functions. The consecration by a bishop of a particular individual as a priest was "just as if in the name of the whole congregation he took one person out of the community, *each member of which has equal power* [italics mine] and commanded him to exercise this power for the rest. . . . " Luther put great emphasis on this point. He offered a story in illustration. If "ten pious Christian laymen" were carried off into the desert as prisoners and had not in their number a priest, they would, in such circumstances, be entirely free to elect one of their number, "born in wedlock or not," and instruct him to "baptize, to celebrate the mass, to absolve, and to preach." Such an individual would be a priest "as truly . . . as if all the bishops and all the popes had consecrated him. . . . For, since we are all priests alike, no man may put himself forward or take upon himself, without our consent and election, to that which we have all alike power to do." This was about as revolutionary and egalitarian as it was possible to get, and Luther dwelt almost lovingly on a point that could not have gone down very well with his noble readers.

Doubtlessly influenced by Augustine, Luther placed great emphasis on the issue of justice. Justice must above all be evenhanded. As things stood, if a priest was killed, a whole country might be "laid under an interdict," that is to say, suffer general excommunication. If a priest, "why not also if a peasant is killed. Whence comes this great difference among equal Christians?"

Having demonstrated to his own satisfaction the fallacy of the superiority of the spiritual power over the temporal (the first wall), Luther went on to examine the proposition that only the pope could interpret Scripture. Here again he displayed his polemical skills, moving easily from satire and ridicule to closely reasoned argument. Where in Scripture could be found the authority for a pope to exercise such a power? The fact was that there were many pious Christians who "have the true faith, spirit, understanding, word, and mind of Christ,'' and why should we then ''reject their word and understanding, and follow a pope who has neither understanding nor spirit?'' If the pope were the final authority on all matters having to do with the faith, should not Christians then say, ''I believe in the Pope of Rome,'' instead of ''I believe in the holy Christian Church''?

The third wall protecting the Church of Rome from criticism or reform was the doctrine that only the pope had the power to call councils to discuss and adjudicate ecclesiastical controversies. Here Luther was at his harshest. Any group of Christians could call a council and if the pope tried to prevent it, he should be ignored. If he ''should begin to excommunicate and fulminate, we must despise this as the doings of a madman, and, trusting in God, excommunicate and repel him as best we may.''

Excommunicate the pope! Strong talk indeed. Having demolished the ''three walls'' and indeed left hardly one stone on another, Luther went on to make clear his determination to call a council and write its agenda.

In his essay on ''Christian Liberty,'' Luther dwells at length on the paradox that the Christian ''is the most free lord of all, and subject to none,'' while, at the same time, ''the most dutiful servant of all, and subject to everyone.'' Truly free in the Lord and truly the servant, that is the faithful Christian. ''We conclude therefore that a Christian man does not live in himself, but in Christ and in his neighbours, or else is no Christian: in Christ by faith; in his neighbour by love. By faith he is carried upwards above himself to God, and by love he sinks back below himself to his neighbour, still always abiding in God and His love. . . . ''

The greater part of ''Christian Liberty'' is taken up with arguments for justification by faith rather than by works. In Luther's view, the fatal flaw in the Church's doctrine of salvation through works was that it opened the door to such abuses as the sale of indulgences and a kind of bartering between the Church and rich patrons. If a patron would pay, often a very large sum, to build or adorn a chapel or a monastery, that patron could be assured of salvation. The doctrine of works was thus used, as political campaign contributions are today, to buy favors from power.

Luther charged the ''Romish Church'' with tolerating usury (Florence in the middle of the fifteenth century had seventy-two banks). ''Truly,'' he wrote, ''this usury is a sign and warning that the world has been given over to the devil for its sins, and that we are losing our spiritual and temporal welfare alike; yet we heed it not.'' Commerce in general, Luther believed, should be discouraged in favor of agriculture; ''they do the best who, according to the Scriptures, till the ground to get their living.'' These observations of Luther's on usury are worth noting in light of Max Weber's theory that a more tolerant attitude on the part of Protestantism toward commercial activity paved the way for capitalism. The fact is that all the reformers were suspicious of business or commercial activity and, like Luther, favored agricultural life.

There was a kind of down-to-earth practicality in Luther that showed clearly in his attack on the requirement for priestly celibacy: "There is many a poor priest free from blame in all other respects," Luther wrote, "except that he has succumbed to human frailty and come to shame with a woman, both minded in their hearts to live together always in conjugal fidelity," if only the Church by its prohibition of marriage had not turned them into hypocrites and sinners.

Not to allow priests to marry was to subject them, in most instances, to the most terrible temptations, to force them to live in sin, married in the eyes of the Lord but concealing and denying the relationship with untold suffering to the women with whom they lived and the children of such unions. "My advice," Luther wrote, "is to restore liberty, and to leave every man [priest] free to marry or not to marry." Priests should rebel against such "devilish tyranny." An oath of chastity should not be exacted, for "human frailty does not allow men to live an unmarried life" but only "angelic fortitude and celestial virtue."

Luther was especially critical of the universities where, he declared, Aristotle was worshiped and the Scriptures ignored. The fact was that centuries of trying to reconcile Aristotle with Christian doctrine had proved fruitless. "Besides," Luther added, "no one has been able to understand his meaning, and much time has been wasted and many noble souls vexed with much useless labour, study and expenses. . . . My heart is grieved to see how many of the best Christians this accursed, proud, knavish heathen has fooled and led astray with his false words. God sent him as a plague for our sins.''

The fact was that, in the universities, ''nothing is considered but numbers, and every man wishes to have a Doctor's title. . . .'' Luther declared himself in favor of establishing schools where young boys could learn the Gospel, ''and would to God,'' Luther added, ''each town had also a girls' school in which girls might be taught the Gospels for an hour daily, either in German or Latin.''

With Luther's Theses it became clear that the pod of revolution was ready to burst throughout Europe. It may well have been that the difference between the earlier movements of Wyclif and Hus and the explosion that followed Luther's defiance of Rome was to be found in the evolution of the printing press. Developed some sixty years earlier, it offered a technology that enabled a printer to turn out pamphlets with comparative speed. The Theses were printed in Wittenberg, and it has been estimated that within a few weeks virtually every literate German had read them and those who could not read had had them read to them. By 1523, eight years after Luther's initial action, more than thirteen hundred different editions of Luther's writings had been published, an astonishing number.

Much of the influence of Luther was the result of his considerable gifts as a writer and polemicist as well as of the dramatic character of his own life. He married an aristocratic ex-nun, Catherine von Bora; the couple had six children and adopted four orphans. The circumstances of their meeting were dramatic enough. Twelve nuns from a convent near Wittenberg appealed to Luther to help them leave the cloistered life. He readily complied. In the words of a young Wittenberger: "A wagon load of vestal virgins has just come to town, all more eager for marriage than for life. God grant them husbands lest worse befall." Luther found husbands for all but Catherine, so he married her himself.

"There is a lot to get used to in the first year of marriage," he wrote. "One wakes up in the morning and finds a pair of pigtails which were not there before."

Delighted with the married state, he even wrote a treatise, *Concerning the Married Life*, in which he offers a dialogue between Reason and Christian Faith. Reason: "Why must I rock the baby, wash its nappies, change its bed, smell its odour, heal its rash? It is better to remain single and lead a quiet and carefree life. I will become a priest or a nun and tell my children to do the same."

To this Christian Faith replies: "The father opens his eyes, looks at these lowly, distasteful and despised things and knows that they are adorned with divine approval as with the most precious gold and silver. God, with his angels and creatures, will smile—not because nappers are washed, but because it is done in faith."

Like Wyclif and Hus before him, Luther believed that it was essential to translate the Bible into the language of the ordinary believer. If salvation could come, not through the intervention of priest and bishops but only through the reading and study of the Holy Scriptures, it followed as the night the day that the faithful had the strongest of incentives to become literate—the desire for salvation. That one principle—the principle that the Christian was justified not through rituals and formularies, but by his or her faith—made possible the modern world. Such belief not only made it possible; it made it inevitable.

Luther's authority extended no further, of course, than his own personal influence, which in the main was confined to Germany. But his ideas, as distinguished from his personal leadership, knew no limits. They flowed like water wherever the protesting spirit manifested itself, and this was especially true of his teachings about equality, "every man a priest and king."

The determination of the Reformers to penetrate the other world was one of the decisive episodes in history. The remarkable thing about it was that that determination was so widespread and so deep. There were no conclaves, councils, conferences; it was as though that steely, undeflectable determination rose out of the collective Christian subconscious, as we like to say today.

If Luther was the dramatic leader of the Reformation in Germany, John Calvin, a Frenchman who established his headquarters in Geneva, was the most influential in the emerging European countries and in England. Born in 1509, Calvin was twenty-six years Luther's junior. After studying law and theology at Bourges, Calvin went on to Paris to study the classics and theology. In 1533, he experienced a "sudden conversion" to the major principles of the Reformation and began work on a vast systematic review of protesting doctrine, the *Institutes of the Christian Religion*. In the *Institutes* Calvin laid out what were to become the theological foundations of the reformed faith in virtually every Protestant country. Published in Latin and French, it was soon translated into High Dutch, Low Dutch, Italian, Spanish, and English, in which latter country it went rapidly through six editions.

To Calvin, the doctrine essential to the reformed churches was justification by faith. That basic doctrine undercut at once the whole immense hierarchy of the Roman Church and asserted the democratic principle that came to characterize Protestantism in all its various sects and denominations. Simply put, the individual believer was directly responsible to his/her Maker, the Lord of the universe. By the same token any company of believers was made up of individuals equal in the eyes of the Lord and possessing power over their own ecclesiastical affairs. They were free to institute their own local church and choose their own pastor. We talk today about "empowering" this or that group that lacks the political or social influence to make their needs felt in the larger political context. The doctrine of justification by faith was the greatest "empowerment" in history. If we keep in mind that power in the sixteenth century resided almost exclusively in the hands of land-owning aristocrats and nobles, emperors, kings and princes, and, of course, the omnipresent Roman Church, we can get some notion of how radical a challenge the Reformers posed to the status quo.

If the individual believer was justified by faith, it followed that "the guidance and teaching of the Scripture [was] necessary to lead to the knowledge of God the Creator." We hardly need dwell on the revolutionary force of this proposition. As we have noted, if salvation of one's soul depends on being able to read and interpret Scripture, the incentive to read is suddenly overwhelming.

Not surprisingly, Calvin has a good deal to say on the doctrine of original sin. The doctrine, Calvin points out, is uncongenial to us. We prefer to think of ourselves as good, rather than to face "our miserable poverty and ignominy, which ought to overwhelm us with shame. For there is nothing more desired by the human mind than soothing flatteries; and therefore it listens with extreme credulity to hear its excellence magnified. . . . For, an immoderate self-love being innate in all men, they readily persuade themselves that there is nothing in them which justly deserves to be an object of aversion."

Here, indeed, is the hinge of the matter between the city of God and the city of man. The inhabitants of the city of man are confident that they are sufficient unto themselves. They need acknowledge no higher power, no principles other than those they have devised. Pride and disobedience to the Lord were Adam's sins; not eating a particular piece of fruit or yielding to the seductions of Eve. At the heart of Adam's disobedience was vanity and presumption, the desire to place himself on the same level as the Almighty One. His punishment and that of his progeny through all generations were the "dreadful pests of ignorance, impotence, impurity, vanity, and iniquity. This is that hereditary corruption which the Father called *original sin*."

Calvin also stresses the necessity for austerity, for the practice of self-denial, since the material things of the world pose a constant threat to the believer, tempting him/her to make them gods: "To desire wealth and honours, to be ambitious of power, to accumulate riches, to amass all these vanities which appear conducive to magnificence and pomp, our passion is furious, and our cupidity unbounded. . . . Hence we may see how restless the minds of those persons are, who regulate their lives according to their own reason. . . . " To live simply and austerely, to care for others and minister to the needy is to bear the cross that Christ bore. In Calvin's words: "When the Scripture enjoins us to discard all private and selfish considerations, it not only erases from our minds the cupidity of wealth, the lust of power, and the favour of men, but also eradicates ambition and all appetites after human glory." It is in denial of the worldly that the Christian possesses his or her soul and this spirit of self-denial, once obtained, "leaves room neither for pride, haughtiness or ostentation, nor for avarice, libidinousness, luxury, effeminacy, or any other evils which are the offspring of self-love."

This emphasis on austerity and self-denial is often

pointed to by critics of the protesting faith as evidence of an inherent hostility to the joys and pleasures of an abundant life to which the faithful would certainly reply that true joy and freedom came, as Calvin argued, not from an accumulation of worldly goods but from a disciplined and pious heart. The joy was not in the material things but in transcending them in the service of the Lord.

Indeed, Calvin was at pains to make clear that God had created the world for the use and the wise stewardship of his creatures. Again, in Calvin's words: "The Scripture . . . fully instructs us in the right use of terrestrial blessings. . . ." If our "present life," our life on earth, is "a pilgrimage toward the celestial kingdom, it is nonetheless the case that the Lord expects us to make such a use of its blessings as will rather assist than retard us in our journey." Good and holy men, conscious of the pitfalls that lie in wait for the pious, have sometimes erred on the side of extreme asceticism, denying the manifold joys and delights in which the world abounds. Calvin cited, as an example of this extreme, Crates the Theban, who threw all his wealth into the sea in the fear that unless it was destroyed, he himself would be destroyed by it. "It must be laid down as a principle," Calvin continued, "that the use of the gifts of God is not erroneous when it is directed to the same end for which the Creator himself has created and appointed them for us; since he has created them for our benefit, not for our injury [but] . . . for our pleasure and delight." Conversely, the faithful should "perpetually and resolutely exert themselves to retrench all superfluities and to restrain luxury.''

One of Calvin's principal points is to be found in his discussion of vocation. In order that there be as little confusion and disorder as possible in the lives of the faithful, God has "appointed to all their particular role in different spheres of life. . . . Every individual's line of life, therefore, is, as it were, a post assigned to him by the Lord, that he may not wander about in uncertainty all his days.'' Furthermore, there is no vocation or calling more honorable in the eyes of the Lord than another. The work of the street cleaner is no less respectable than that of the preacher or doctor of laws, providing always that such tasks are performed as a mode of worship of the Lord's goodness and benignity. In the words of the Puritan poet George Herrick, "who sweeps a room as for thy laws, makes that and the action fine." It is not the task but the spirit in which it is performed that has value in the eyes of the Lord. "Hence . . . will arise peculiar consolation, since there will be no employment so mean and sordid . . . as not to appear truly respectable, and be deemed highly important in the sight of God,'' what we might call the democratization of work, an essential prerequisite of political democracy.

In the years that followed the publication of Luther's tracts and Calvin's *Institutes*, the issues raised by the Reformers became intensely political. Kings and princes favored the reformers or, conversely, the Roman Church, largely in terms of their political interests. This prince, confident in his alliance with a king or emperor favorably inclined to the reformers (usually because they strengthened his hand in a contest with Rome and her allies), would give his support to the Lutheran faction or, somewhat later, to the Calvinists. And of course, there were often sharp divisions among the reformers themselves, as was the case with the Hussites and the Lutherans, and, in England, the advocates of the Church of England and the radical Protestant sects, the Presbyterians, the Independents, and a half-dozen even more radical parties.

In the words of the British economic historian R. H. Tawney, "Where Lutherianism had been socially conservative, deferential to established political authorities, the exponent of a personal, almost quietistic, piety, Calvinism was an active and radical force. It was a creed which sought, not merely to purify the individual, but to reconstruct Church and State, and to renew society by penetrating every department of life, public as well as private, with the influence of religion." In other words, Calvin and his followers wanted the city of God not only to lay the city of man under judgment—or, where possible, to cooperate with it—not only to seek to tame its most untidy passions, but in fact to supersede it.

4

COMMUNITIES OF
THE LORD

Calvin's *Institutes*, as has been noted, was especially congenial to the English protesters against the authority and, even more important, the theology of Rome. In an astonishingly short time, from the late 1500s through the early 1600s, England was filled, it seemed, with radical Christians protesting every form of authority, civil or ecclesiastical. Those who dissented from the state church, the Church of England, established by Henry VIII, hoped to reform the church along Calvinist lines. Other groups had humbler expectations. They simply wished to separate from the Church of England and be left to live and worship after their own fashion.

A group of the latter left England early in the seventeenth century, hoping to find a more congenial atmosphere among the congregations of the Dutch Reformed (Calvinistic) Church. In 1620, a band of these refugees, concerned that their children were in danger of becoming Hollandized, or Dutchified, decided to undertake the hazardous venture of ''planting'' themselves on a portion of the land that had been granted by the British crown to the New England Company. In the words of one member of the company, "Of all the sorowes [suffered in Holland] most heavie to be borne, was that many of their children, by these occasions, and the great licentiousness of the youth in that countrie, and the manifold temptations of the place were drawne away by evil examples into extravagant and dangerous courses, putting the reines off their nekes and parting from their parents. . . . "

As every schoolchild knows, or used to know, these "pilgrims" landed at a spot on the harsh New England coast that they called Plymouth, after the English town of that name.

On the way over on the *Mayflower*, the passengers drew up an agreement or "compact" subsequently celebrated as the "Mayflower Compact" and usually credited with being the Ur document of American democracy. There was, of course, a practical reason for drawing up such an agreement. In addition to the true believers, the Brownists, or Separatists—the "saints" (saints in the sense that all the faithful were saints)—there were in the company some "strangers," some men and women who were not in communion, who gave their allegiance to the Church of England or to no church at all. So it was simply prudent to get everyone to agree on the source of authority for the colony: the congregation of the saints.

This all seems today unremarkable enough but it was, for the time, an extraordinary assertion of power by simple people who had always experienced power as something "outside"—the power of the Church of England and its priests and bishops, power in the form of edicts of the Crown and its officials, or in the statutes of Parliament. So that to even imagine that they could state out of their own free will, out of the freedom that they enjoyed as partakers of God's freedom, the terms of their governance was astonishing and instructive. It may have been the first time any group of simple, ordinary people had found the courage and enterprise to do such a thing, and thus deserves to be noted and honored and remembered.

We know of the hardships and sufferings of the Pilgrims because they were fortunate enough to have a master historian to tell their story. William Bradford's *History of the Plymouth Plantation* is one of the great narratives of our history. After giving his account of the voyage to New England, Bradford wrote:

> Here I cannot but pause and stand amazed, and so, too, I think will the reader when he considers this poor people and their present condition. For they had no dwelling places for their weather-beaten bodies, no houses or much less towns to repair to, to seek for succor. And for the season, it was winter, and they that know the winters of that country know them to be sharp and violent, and subject to cruel and fierce storms, dangerous to travel to known places, much more to search an unknown coast. Besides what could they see but a hideous and desolate wilderness, full of

wild beasts and wild men—and what multitudes
there might be of them they knew not. Neither
could they, as it were, go to the top of Pisgah
to view from the wilderness a more goodly country to feed their hopes; for which way soever
they turned their eyes (save upwards to the heav-
ens) they would have little solace or content in
respect of any outward objects. For summer
being done, all things stand upon them with a
weatherbeaten face, and the whole country full
of woods and thickets, represented a wild and
savage hue. . . . If they looked behind them,
there was the mighty ocean over which they had
passed and was now a main bar and gulf to
separate them from all the civil parts of the
world. . . . What could now sustain them but the
spirit of God and His Grace?

The first Indians that the Pilgrims encountered were mem-
bers of the Wampanoag tribe. To their astonishment, an
Indian named Samoset greeted them in broken English
and introduced them to another English-speaking Indian,
Squanto, who became their particular friend and adviser.
In turn they met Massasoit, the sachem, or chief, of the
Wampanoags, and concluded a peace that remained intact
for fifty years.

Appealing as the story of the Pilgrims is, it is only a
footnote to the much larger emigration ten years later by
Englishmen who called themselves Puritans. They were

a more prosperous, better educated company; a number of their leaders were graduates of Cambridge in a day when only a handful of upper-class Englishmen attended Oxford or Cambridge. The motives of the Puritans in coming to a "New" England were very different from those of their predecessors. The Puritans considered themselves members of the Church of England and their intention was, as we have noted, to reform the church. Indeed, so powerful were the Puritans in their several manifestations that in another decade they would challenge the Church of England and its allies for the control of the British Parliament and, indeed, for rule of the country itself. What troubled the reformers in England was what we might call the ubiquitousness of the city of man. Great Britain was a great nation, one of the principal powers in the world with "global interests," as we would say today. As members of a rising commercial nation, many of its citizens had accumulated great wealth, and the Church of England was the state church in close alliance with the crown and the nobles of the land. To establish the city of God in competition with the city of man was a formidable task. Meanwhile, it was tempting to try the experiment of a Bible Commonwealth in an uncontaminated environment, so to speak, to establish a community or congery of communities where the true principles of the reformed faith could be put into practice without the worldly distractions and compromises that would have beset any such venture in England itself.

The Separatists had prospered modestly, demonstrating that some semblance of civilized life was possible even in the inhospitable climate of New England. Plans were thus drawn up for a great migration of the faithful, the saints (accompanied to be sure by some nonsaints, or ordinary run-of-the-mill sinners) to found the city of God in a fresh "new world." It was an exhilarating prospect. For the first time since the days of the primitive Christian Church, a true egalitarian Christian democracy would be established that would in time demonstrate to the whole of Christendom that the city of God could, in fact, be established on earth. The notion was so alluring that hundreds and soon thousands of prosperous and prominent Englishmen and women were ready to abandon all that was familiar and beloved, hearth and home, friends, public offices and future prospects, for an uncertain venture in an unknown land. One of the leaders of the first band of settlers was John Winthrop, member of the gentry and a graduate of Cambridge. On board the *Arabella*, headed for the coast of New England, Winthrop drew up a kind of spiritual charter for the enterprise. He entitled it *A Model of Christian Charity*. In it were echoes of the early Church, as well, of course, as Augustine's *City of God*. The prescription was clear enough. The mission was to create the true community, knit together by Christian love. It was God's intention that "every man might have need of other, and from hence they might all be knit more nearly together in the bonds of brotherly affection." The Puritans had a special covenant with the Lord for the work that they were undertaking. If they arrived safely in New England, it would be a sign that the Lord had ratified the covenant. What this meant was that they were under the sternest injunctions to live up to the exacting terms of their agreement. If they failed to do so and became distracted by the temptations of the flesh and the distractions of the city of man, they would, it followed, be severely punished by the Lord, who would "make us know the price of a breach of such a covenant."

The only way to avoid the wrath of the Lord was to follow the exortation of Micah, "To do justly, to love mercy, to walk humbly with our God." This required that "we must be knit together in this work as one man. . . . We must hold familiar commerce together in meekness, gentleness, patience, and liberality. We must delight in each other; make each other's conditions our own, rejoice together, having always before our eyes our commission and community in the work, our community as members of the same bond. . . . We shall find that the God of Israel is among us. . . when He shall make us a praise and glory that men shall say of succeeding plantations 'the Lord make it like that of NEW ENGLAND!' For we must consider that we shall be as a city upon a hill. The eyes of all people are upon us."

The practical documents—the "covenants"—stating the intentions of each community, reflected the spirit of Winthrop's tract. That of Braintree was typical: "With God's help the signers mean to renounce the devil, the wicked world, a sinful flesh . . . and all our former evil ways . . . and we give up ourselves also to one another by the will of God . . . and we also manifest our joint consent herein this day in the presence of this assembly, by this present our public confession, and by giving one another the hand of fellowship.''

It was, of course, essential that the physical arrangement of the Puritan township reflect the principles of Christian democracy and equality. In regard to the communitarian, or communist, character of the town, all its members should be as nearly equal in property as possible and hold the rest of the township in ''common.'' Hence the town faced the town common, the common property of all. Each member of the community had a town lot and a farm lot outside of town, each chosen by lot. In addition, there was a common woodlot where all might get firewood. The actual plan of the town was not entirely an invention of the settlers; it had its original in the medieval English village where much the same ethic of land use prevailed for centuries. The point to emphasize about the New England town that we still cherish as an ideal of democracy was that in it was bred the experience of self-government that rested essentially on the assurance of God's liberty. The ''individual'' had such power and confidence as never before, if we except the primitive church. The power was derived not from the individual per se, who indeed was quite powerless, but from his or her membership in the faithful community. In such communities women also had a new dignity and status. The symbol of this elevation of women was to be found in the person of Anne Hutchinson, who formed a schismatic group made up of some of the most influential members of the Bible Commonwealth and set up a colony of her own at Portsmouth in what became Rhode Island.

Simply put, there was no place in the overwhelmingly small-town, rural life of the English colonies for any hint of "capitalism," by whatever definition. If covenanted communities of New England (and many of the Middle States) were the archetype, there were, of course, variations. But for almost a hundred and fifty years, covenanted communities dominated colonial life and so impressed themselves on our collective consciousness that we have never ceased to look back to them as representing the high point in the American dream of equality and democracy. Their image is preserved in hundreds of little "museums," New England towns that still enact these ancient rituals, summoning up the ghosts of meetings long past.

The essence of the Protestant community was, as we have noted, the congregation. No priest or bishop, or synod, made the decisions governing the life of the community—these were made by the congregations, hence in time called Congregationalists. When they met to carry on the governance of the community (in the same meeting house), they were the civil government.

There was, to be sure, commercial activity in the seacoast towns but little or no industry, and some merchant families prospered notably, thereby giving substance to

John Wesley's concern that thrift and hard work must lead inevitably to riches, dissipation, and the decline in religion (although the latter was little to be noticed in most seaport towns), and confirming the suspicion in rural towns that "cities" were the playground of the devil.

Not only was there little incentive to develop the instrumentalities of what might be called capitalism (large-scale capital accumulation for manufacturing or mining enterprises), the colonists were under specific injunctions not to engage in any activity that might compete with the interests of the mother country. Great Britain and her principal rivals—Spain, Holland, and France—were under the spell of mercantilism, a subdivision of capitalism that held that the role of colonies was to provide raw material for the manufactures of the mother country and in turn to consume the finished products of these factories. What the mother country, under the theory of mercantilism, wished to avoid at all costs was competition from its colonies. Trade, like frigates and canons, was an instrument of national policy. Trade must be used as a weapon to weaken rival nations.

Certainly, many of these prohibitions rankled the colonists. Tea, for example, could only be carried in English-owned vessels. The colonists were not allowed to cut any pine trees that had been marked with the insignia of the royal navy. Whenever some modest colonial enterprise threatened a real or fancied interest, Parliament would place it under a ban. This sense of subordination disturbed many colonists. But the point to emphasize is that such irritants were relatively minor and the vast majority of colonists were self-sufficient farmers.

5

THE GREAT REBELLION

While the English colonies carried on their "errand into the wilderness," their cousins in the motherland, the reformers and radical protesters, were shaking the nation to its very foundation.

On the death in 1603 of Queen Elizabeth, the Virgin Queen with no heirs, James VI of Scotland became James I, King of England, the first of the Stuart line. Dogmatic and highhanded, and Scottish in addition, James soon found himself embroiled in disputes with Parliamentary leaders, a number of whom were ardent dissenters who called themselves nonconformists in regard to the Church of England. James was unyielding. "No Bishop, No King," he declared, adding, "I shall make them conform themselves or I will harry them out of the land."

The contest between the king and the nonconformists centered in the House of Commons. Under the religious impulse, the leaders of Parliament became master politicians, employing a wide range of strategies to define and limit the prerogatives of the king. They declared that the House of Commons was "the sole proper judge" of the actions of its members and of the terms under which they were elected. "The rights and liberties of the Commons of England consisteth chiefly in these three things," the petition continued: "first, that the shires, cities, and boroughs of England . . . have free choice of such persons as they shall put in trust to represent them"; second, that such persons should be free from arrest or retraint during the sessions of Parliament; and "thirdly, that in Parliament they may speak freely their conscience without check and controlment."

To which James replied that he considered himself "very free and able to punish any man's misdemeanors in Parliament, as well during their sitting as after. . . ." He would tolerate no man's "insolent behavior."

The reply of Parliament is one of our historic political documents. Known as the Great Protestation, it began:

> The Commons now assembled in Parliament, being justly [concerned about] . . . sundry liberties, franchises, and privileges, do make this protestation following: that the liberties, franchises, privileges, and jurisdictions of Parliament are the ancient and undoubted birthright and inheritance of the subjects of England; and that the arduous and urgent affairs concerning the king, state, and defense of the realm and of the Church of England, and the maintenance and making of the laws, and the redress of mis-

chiefs and grievances which daily happen within this realm are proper subjects and matter of counsel and debate in Parliament; and that . . . every member . . . hath and of right ought to have freedom of speech, to propound, treat, reason, and bring to conclusion the same; and that the Commons in Parliament have the like liberty and freedom to treat of these matters . . . as in their judgments shall seem fittest; and that every member of the said house hath like freedom from all impeachment, imprisonment, and molestation . . . for or concerning any speaking, reasoning, or declaring of any matter or matters touching the Parliament or Parliament business. . . .

With James in constant contention with Parliament, Britain's role in European affairs steadily diminished. When James died in 1625, England was at a low ebb. The succession of his son, Charles I, who was married to Henrietta Maria, a French Catholic, only made matters worse. Charles was as stubborn as his father, and more ambitious. He initiated military ventures (usually inept) that required large sums to finance, and when he called Parliament into session he was confronted by their demands. In 1629, after a particularly bitter confrontation, Charles dissolved Parliament, which did not meet again for eleven years. Meanwhile, the king had the leader of Parliament, Sir John Eliot, arrested and placed in the

Tower of London, where he died rather than recant his criticisms of the king's misuse of the royal prerogative.

In 1638, Scotland revolted, successfully routed a royal army, and invaded England. Charles, confident that Parliament would rally to the royal standard in the face of the threat from the north, called Parliament into session. Contrary to his expectations, Parliament at once began drawing up petitions protesting the king's abuse of his powers. Charles promptly prorogued Parliament, but it reassembled on its own and, in effect, undertook to run the country. For two years the more moderate elements among the Puritans (termed Roundheads because they cut their hair short and scorned the fashionable wigs of the day) joined forces with those adherents of the Church of England who were anxious to find a middle ground. Charles was the principal stumbling block. His response to the recalcitrance of Parliament was to attempt to arrest its leaders for treason. And *their* response was to appoint an extra-legal body entitled the committee for public safety and muster an army of twenty thousand citizen-soldiers supplemented by four thousand calvary. The king, in turn, called on the badly demoralized royal army.

The first encounter between the two armies was some-what in favor of the royalist forces, but before the king and his allies could exploit their advantage, a group of strongly Puritan counties raised a contingent of their own and placed it under the command of a man who proved to be one of the geniuses of modern warfare. Oliver

Cromwell was a natural leader. He cured his motley force of the plague of irregulars, lack of discipline, and made them into a formidable fighting force, soon known as Cromwell's Ironsides and the New Model Army. The Parliamentary army administered a decisive defeat to Charles's forces at Marston Moor in July 1644. Edward Hyde, Earl of Clarendon and historian of the rebellion, wrote of Cromwell's army that it had "great discipline, diligence and sobriety; which begat courage and resolution in them, and notable dexterity in achievements and enterprises." The Royalists, on the other hand, fell into "license, disorder and impiety," so that one side seemed "to fight for monarchy with the weapons of confusion, and the other to destroy the King and government with all the principles and regularity of monarchy."

Charles now formed an alliance with the Scots who invaded England in August 1648, and were met and decisively defeated by Cromwell at the Battle of Preston. The king was captured, tried before a high court appointed by Parliament, sentenced to death and beheaded at Whitehall on January 30, 1649. It was the first civil war in modern times in which a ruling monarch had been defeated in a popular uprising and, most horrendous of all, executed. The event sent a shock wave through every monarchy in Europe. Parliament declared the nation no longer a monarchy, but now a "Commonwealth," and for eleven years ruled over a bitterly divided nation, sustained primarily by Cromwell and his army. The nation was fortunate in Cromwell, who called himself the "constable of the people," and while acting as a virtual dictator, avoided all the trappings of power and showed as much skill in conciliation as he had in arms. His official title was Lord Protector of the Commonwealth of England, Scotland, and Ireland. His powers were defined by the first written constitution in modern history, entitled Instrument of Government.

The social and political chaos that resulted from the toppling of the Crown brought to the surface long-smoldering class resentments. These took the form, in the main, of radical Christian protestations that traced their lineage through the constantly suppressed Lollards to John Wyclif himself; a wild profusion of Christian communisms competed for the soul of the nation.

The Fifth Monarchy men were millenarians. They expected the imminent return of Christ to reign on earth a thousand years. That would be the "fifth" monarchy. According to their interpretation of the Book of Daniel, there had been four earlier monarchies—the Assyrian, Persian, Greek, and Roman. The city of God must now be established by force, if necessary, in anticipation of the millennium. When a plot by Fifth Monarchy men to assassinate Cromwell was unearthed, a number of the members of the group were imprisoned.

The radical pamphleteer Gerrard Winstanley denounced the various Parliamentary Protestants—the Baptists, Independents, Presbyterians chiefly among them—for not being willing to carry social reform far enough. "What stock," Winstanley asked, "is provided for the *poor, fatherless, widows*, and *impoverished people?* And what advancement or encouragement for the *laboring* and *industrious*, as to take off their burthen is there?'' Winstanley went so far as to argue that the earth should be made *"a common Treasury of livelihood to whole mankind, without respect of persons,"* a restatement of the classic Christian dream of a world where everything was held in common. The *Community of Mankind*, the first primitive Christian community, was made up of all those joined in "the unity of the spirit of Love, which is called Christ in you, or the Law written in the heart, leading mankind unto all truth, and to be of one heart and one mind." The second community was the *"Community of the Earth*, for the quiet livelihood in food and raiment without using force or restraining one another."

The earth, Winstanley insisted, "must be set free from the intanglements of Lords and Landlords, and that it shall become a common treasury to all, as it was first given to the sonnes of men," and "not only this Common, or Heath should be taken in and Manured by the People, but all the Commons and waste Ground in . . . the whole world." As the literary historian Don Wolfe has put it, Winstanley proposed "a communistic state without buying and selling, without money, without tithes, without hereditary titles, without inequality of income, to be governed democratically by sufferage of all men over twenty including drunkards and sinful people. . . . ''

In April 1649, Winstanley and four of his followers went to St. George's Hill in Surrey and started to dig up the earth and plant beans, carrots, and parsnips. Six months later some fifty others had joined. They dug and planted in common unclaimed lands but they nonetheless aroused the fury of their neighbors, who attacked and beat them, destroyed their tools, and pulled up their crops. Winstanley and a number of his followers were arrested for trespass, an event that prompted one of his most famous tracts, *A Watch-Word to the City of London, and the Armie, Wherein You May see that England's free-dome, which should be the result of all our Victories, is sinking deeper under the Norman power, as appears by this relation of the unrighteous proceedings of the King-stone-Court against some of the Diggers at George-Hill, under colour of Law* . . . (to give the incomplete title).

John Lilburne, like Luther, believed that God, "the absolute Soveraign Lord and King," had created men and women "by nature all equall and alike in power, dignity, authority and majesty, none of them having (by nature) any authority dominion or majesteriall power, one over or above another . . . without their free consent."

Compared to Winstanley, John Lilburne was a model of moderation. While he and his followers wanted to introduce a general social levelling in society (hence "Levellers"), they were careful to distance themselves from the Diggers. John Lilburne, who was an officer in the New Model Army and a friend of Cromwell, devoted the greater part of his more than two hundred pamphlets to attacking the institution of kingship and pressing for more democratic reform than Cromwell and Parliament generally were willing to agree to.

When Cromwell died in 1658, the nation faced another crisis. The rickety nature of the joint rule of Parliament and Cromwell was exposed by the issue of succession. It was decided that Cromwell's inept son Richard, derisively called "Tumble-Down Dick," should succeed him, but two years of Richard Cromwell gave Parliament a bellyful. The moderates in Parliament now held the balance of power and decided, after much agonizing, to restore the Stuart monarchy by calling Charles II, son of the beheaded king, to the throne of England, Scotland, and Ireland.

The English Civil War can properly claim to be the first of a series of modern revolutions that literally transformed the world. What distinguished it from the common run of civil wars, of which there had been and were to be more than a sufficiency, was that it set out to map a whole new political realm having to do with the relations of a people to its government.

With the ascention of Charles II to the throne, it seemed to those Englishmen of the dissenting persuasion that everything they had fought for through some twenty bloody and chaotic years had been lost as the nation gave itself over to a period of licentiousness and self-indulgence. It was as though the supporters of the monarchy were determined to outrage every pious precept of their enemies. One result was a considerable stimulus to migration to the new and uncorrupted England across the ocean.

It is hard at this remove in time to appreciate fully the impact on the modern world of the Great Rebellion—or the English Civil War or, as it is perhaps more commonly, and rather misleadingly, called, the Interregnum. For the first time since classical times, a reigning monarch had been deposed by a popular uprising of "the people," and this uprising had been guided by a Christian ardor that claimed to belong to a tradition that went back to the primitive church. In the words of the British historian George Trevelyan: "[It was] the true turning-point in the political history of the English-speaking races. It not only prevented the English monarchy from hardening into an absolutism of the type then becoming general in Europe, but it made a great experiment in direct rule of the country and the Empire by the House of Commons." Beyond that it released into the arena of public discourse notions of radical reform that challenge us today. In more specifically political terms, it laid out a series of propositions concerning the rights and privileges of Englishmen that were instantly transplanted to the British colonies in North America and there grew as luxuriantly as weeds.

After a decade or so of the Restoration, it became clear that the party must end someday. When Charles formed an alliance with England's traditional enemy, Catholic France, for a joint assault on Protestant Holland, he lost much of his support. Had the English people known of a secret clause in the Anglo-French treaty that committed Louis XIV to supply Charles with men and money in order to force Catholicism on that nation, the result would likely have been another uprising. When Charles died in 1685 he was succeeded by his brother, James, a devout Roman Catholic. James quickly alienated a Parliament favorable to monarchy and anxious, above all else, to avoid another plunge into the abyss of civil war, by pressing the Catholic cause remorselessly. The birth of an heir, which raised the question of a Catholic succession, brought things to a head. William of Orange and his consort, Mary, were then invited to replace James. When William and Mary landed at Torbay on November 4, 1688, James's following melted away, and that unhappy monarch, doubtlessly mindful of his father's fate (beheaded by the Parliamentary forces in 1649), fled the country. In return for the handsome prize of the throne of England, William agreed to the so-called Revolution Settlement as the condition of office. The very fact that Parliament had invited him in underlined the power of that body vis-à-vis the new monarch.

The Revolution Settlement had the practical effect of ratifying many of the reforms that Parliament had fought for during the reign of Charles I (and exercised during the Interregnum), and had maintained as best they could during the reign of Charles II. The Declaration of Rights specified among other things that no Roman Catholic could ever be sovereign of England. The Bill of Rights, which accompanied it, was even more "historic." It included a number of the provisions that would appear in our own Bill of Rights, notable among them the right to a trial by a jury of one's peers in the "vicinage," or neighborhood; freedom of speech and assembly; the right to just and equal laws; freedom from self-incrimination; freedom of religion—except, of course, for Catholics. It also provided that no Englishman could henceforth be taxed without his consent as represented in the House of Commons, a provision that subsequently was to prove of some embarrassment to the British.

The point that can't be stressed enough is that those radical Protestants who emigrated, in the main, to New England considered that they carried with them two precious assets. First, they had an opportunity that few Christians had had since the days of the early church to create, free of all distractions and competing social structures, democratic and egalitarian Christian communities—communities of the kind that John Winthrop had written the blueprint for in *A Model of Christian Charity*. Second, and derived directly from the first, they brought with them their political rights as Englishmen as summarized in the Bill of Rights, which were part of the Revolution Settlement. The result was what one might call overlapping jurisdictions between the two cities. The simple, communitarian life of the New England town was, in its larger social and political context as part of the Bible Commonwealth, reinforced by the hard-won rights of the Long Parliament. The same was true, in varying degrees, with all the New England colonies—Connecticut, Rhode Island, and New Hampshire—and, in its own distinctive way, Pennsylvania. The Puritan colonies are sometimes referred to as "theocracies" since Puritan ministers played a central role in their communities, but such a designation is wrong. A theocracy, strictly speaking, means rule by a priestly caste and this was definitely not the case in Puritan New England. The Puritans were careful to distinguish between the two cities. In their towns they met in the meeting house—the church—for worship and for the conduct of the affairs of the church that often had to do with matters of church discipline, including, on occasion, excommunication.

The same individuals met in the meeting house to conduct the practical business of the community—to levy taxes, to elect such unpaid officials as fence-watchers, hog reeves (officials charged with responsibility for stray hogs), and sheriffs.

Since one of the main purposes of this work is to make clear, beyond cavil, that Protestantism, or Puritanism, not only did not create or encourage capitalism but instead did all in its power actively to discourage it by preaching continuously the dangerous temptations of the world, it is worth taking note of the writings of Puritan ministers. Especially since two of the most influential were quoted by Max Weber in support of his thesis.

Richard Baxter (1615–91) served as chaplain in Cromwell's army. Arrested after the restoration of the Stuarts for defaming the Church of England, Baxter was imprisoned for eighteen months by the brutal and sadistic

Judge Jeffreys. Baxter's principal contribution to the dissenting congregations lay in his effort to spell out in considerable detail how the teachings of the city of God should be interpreted by the faithful in their daily lives in the city of man. Baxter's most influential work was titled *Christian Directory, or a Sum of Practical Theologie and Cases of Conscience.* The purpose, as Baxter explained in his introduction, is "the resolving of practical cases of conscience, and the reducing of theoretical knowledge into serious Christian practice." The *Directory* was divided into four parts—Ethics, Economics, Ecclesiastics, and Politics. Baxter, as opposed to, say, John Wyclif, conceded that the city of God must coexist with the city of man. The *Christian Directory* is therefore a highly practical work that proceeds from the assumption that Christians live in a fallen world and need a guidebook in order to find their way through it lest they lose their souls. Baxter urged believers to be honest and industrious workers. "It is for action," he wrote, "that God maintaineth us and our activities. Work is the moral as well as the natural end of power. . . . It is action that God is most served and honored by. . . . The public welfare or the good of many is to be valued above our own." Even the wealthy must work. They have as "great a necessity to obey" as the poor. God has strictly commanded work to all.

"It is not lawful," he wrote, "to take up or keep up any oppressing monopoly or trade, which tends to enrich you by the loss of the commonwealth or of many." The

Christian must carry on his business as a kind of public service. He must not endeavor "to get another's goods or labour for less than it is worth" or try to make a profit "by extortion working upon men's ignorance, error, or necessity." He should offer the poor man "the worth of his commodity and save him from the oppressor." "It is," Baxter notes, "too common a sort of oppression for the rich in all places to domineer too insolently over the poor, and force them to follow their wills and to serve their interest, be it right or wrong." The landlord who takes advantage of the poor and powerless is "an Anti-Christ and an Anti-God . . . not only the agent of the Devil, but his image."

I must say here, parenthetically, that Weber quotes a portion of this same passage and then tells us that it is representative of those Puritan attitudes that *encouraged* the development of modern capitalism. This seems to me tantamount to telling us that black is white.

Second only to the Bible as a source of inspiration to the English settlers in America was John Bunyan's *Pilgrim's Progress*, the story of pious Christian's adventures and mishaps in the city of man.

In Chapter 14 of the first book, having joined forces with Faithful, Christian finds "another excellent companion in Hopeful." Christian and Faithful meet By-ends, a prosperous, comfortable Christian who has no inclination to endure hardships of any kind for his faith. By-ends introduces Christian and Faithful to Money-love. When Money-love is asked if a decision to make money at the expense of principle is consistent with his religious beliefs, he replies in the affirmative. If "by becoming religious" a man can get "a rich wife . . . and good customers, and good gain . . . to get all these is a good and profitable design." To which Christian replies that only "heathens, hypocrites, devils and witches" would make such an unholy bargain.

Another one of Weber's witnesses is John Wesley (1703–91), the founder of Methodism. Wesley constantly warned against the temptation of material things. As for the accumulation of riches, if God shows a way "to make more without danger to your soul or to others," Wesley wrote, "the prudent Christian will take advantage of such an opportunity in order to use God's gifts for the benefit of others." But, under the best of circumstances, the acquisition of wealth was dangerous, for "whenever riches have increased, the essence of religion has decreased in the same proportion . . . as riches increase so will pride, anger, and the love of the world in all its branches." The only way to take the curse off wealth was to "Lay up no treasure on earth, give all that you can, that is, all that you have. I defy all men upon earth, yea all angels in heaven, to find any other way to extract the poison from riches. . . . You who receive 500 pounds a year and spend only 200, do you give back 300 to God? If not, you certainly rob God of that 300." Given the universal human disposition to lay up treasures on earth rather than in heaven, Wesley did not see how it was possible "in the nature of things, for any revival of the true religion to continue long. For religion must necessarily produce the industry and frugality, and these cannot but produce riches. But as riches increase, so will pride, anger, and love of the world in all its branches.''

It seemed to Wesley that the poison of wealth and luxury was already eating away at the heart of the newly founded Methodist denomination. Was there any way to avoid such an outcome, Wesley asked, adding: "We ought not to prevent people from being diligent and frugal; we must exhort all Christians to gain all they can, and to save all they can; that is, in effect, to grow rich.'' Max Weber italicized the last part of the sentence as though it contained the essence of the paragraph. Given the preceding sentences, the last one seems highly ambiguous, a fragile hook to hang a thesis on.

The surprising thing about the challenges to the hegemony of the Roman Church that arose in various parts of Europe at the beginning of the sixteenth century was the fact that the major themes in these assaults on the authority of Rome, were remarkably alike. There were certain basic assumptions common to them all, whether they were manifested by John Wyclif in England, Jan Hus in Bohemia, Martin Luther in Germany, Huldreich Zwingli in Zurich, or John Calvin in Geneva. To call into question the authority of the Church was a frightening exercise. However oppressive and corrupt, the Church still represented the only principle of order and unity *in the world*, or at least in the Western portion of it. Attacking it meant, in effect, opening a Pandora's box of at least potentially widely differing interpretations of Christian doctrine and dogma, not to mention skepticism, agnosticism, and even atheism. Such fractures and schisms did, of course, take place until the fragmenting of the protesting communities became something of a scandal. But when the ecclesiastical dust had settled, what was more remarkable was the affinity among the various sects and denominations rather than their differences. This was doubtlessly due, in large part, to the fact that they had one common enemy, the pope, the Antichrist, the agent of the Devil, as he appeared to all pious reformers.

So there you have it. In theory, in theology, and usually in practice, Protestantism resisted as best it could the rising tide of capitalism. Its commitment was plainly to the Lord and Saviour of the world and to the city of God rather than to the city of man.

Having said all this, having rebutted at some length the notion that Protestantism or Puritanism created "a climate of opinion" that encouraged capitalism, it may be time to make certain concessions. We might put it this way: While the doctrines of the dissenting churches (which became of course in time the dominant denominations) remained unambiguously hostile to capitalism, it was also true that the Reformation unquestionably did provide an important if not an essential boost to the formation of a character type congenial to the development of capitalism, a new kind of human being that came in time to be called an "individual." By shifting the emphasis from salvation through the instrumentalities of the Church to "justification" by the faith of a particular person, an individual, Protestantism gave that particular individual a power that he or she had never had before. It was the power to stand before God. To be, in the slang of today, one-on-one with the Almighty. This new relationship certainly produced vast strains and stresses and proved, in the long run, highly unstable. But at the same time it created remarkable new possibilities. As a member of a faithful community, the individual was supported and sustained by his/her brothers and sisters in a relationship as demanding as it was exalting. That relationship required that the members of the community "internalize" the values of the community. When they left the community, either to found new communities or to make their way in the wider world, they carried these values with them, as much a part of them as their skin or hair. This meant, among other things, that an astonishing range of new combinations was possible, formed not as most such relationships had been formed throughout history—by external forces and powers—but by the free and voluntary linkage of these new individuals with one another. Where economic activities were involved, the effect was often a high degree of efficiency and "speed," what Max Weber presumably means by "rational behavior." What we are talking about here is neither more or less than the "democratization" of capitalism.

Let us try an example. In a traditional society, a "capitalist" venture would typically be initiated by someone with access to power. In fifteenth-century Florence, if someone wished to start a bank, the support of a powerful patron was essential. Ideally, it would be a bishop or cardinal, thereby minimizing the usury problem. Slowly but surely, bourgeois merchants and businessmen forced their way onto the stage but typically it was with the assistance of a patron, an ecclesiastic or a member of the nobility. On the American frontier in the early nineteenth century, half a dozen enterprising pioneers with little or no formal education, no experience in finance, high or low, and no patron, church or lay, could start up a bank. Most, to be sure, went bust shortly but a few survived and flourished. Modern capitalism in general is not based on a high rate of success but rather on a high rate of failure offset by a critical minimum of successes due to luck, persistence, and intelligence.

Finally, there was the matter of time. The Reformation established a new relationship between the individual believer and time. The city of God took time seriously. The Lord had enjoined all of the faithful to make good use of their time, which was their share in God's eternity, and that sense of organizing and being responsible for the wise use of one's time was an important element in the emergence of modern industrial society. Richard Baxter, the Puritan divine, had the same message: "Keep up a high esteem of time and be every day more careful that you lose none of your time than you are that you lose none of your gold and silver. And if vain recreations, dressings, feastings, idle talk, unprofitable company or sleep be any of them temptations to rob you of your time, accordingly heighten your watchfulness.''

In the words of the German sociologist Heinrich Maurer: ''Time had to become God's time before it could become Daylight Savings Time,'' that is, capitalist time.

6

THE ENLIGHTENMENT

Even as the most dramatic manifestation of radical Protestantism was being played out in England in the Great Rebellion that unseated a king and tried the experiment of representative government in the place of monarchy, the prophet of a new secular age was tirelessly at work spelling out his "Method"—a method, he was confident, that could unlock much, if not eventually all, that had been in darkness. René Descartes, born in 1596, was educated at a Jesuit school at La Fleche and at the University of Poitiers. He reacted strongly against the faded scholasticism of his Jesuit training. "I found myself involved in so many doubts and errors," he wrote, "that I was convinced I had advanced no further in all my attempts at learning, than the discovery at every turn of my own ignorance [and, it might be said parenthetically, that of his teachers]. . . . I was thus led to take the liberty of judging all other men by myself, and concluding that there was no science in existence that was of such a nature as I had previously been given to believe." Descartes found the study of mathematics especially congenial. He made important discoveries in that field as well as in the related area of analytical geometry. Indeed his goal, in ranging over the whole field of learning from physics to philosophy, came increasingly to be to apply the principles of mathematics as widely as possible.

He was notably disillusioned with philosophy when it appeared that, although it had been cultivated for many years by "the most distinguished men," there was "not a single matter within its sphere which is not still in dispute. . . . " Disillusioned by the state of scholarship in general, Descartes "resolved no longer to seek any other science than the knowledge of myself, or the great book of the world."

Descartes spent, by his own account, nine years roaming "from one place to another, desirous of being a spectator rather than an actor in the plays exhibited in the theatre of the world."

The starting point of every investigation into the nature of man and the world, Descartes decided, must be to doubt all received knowledge and, starting with the simplest and most obvious observations, build, step-by-step, toward the truth. In his *Discourse on Method*, written toward the end of his relatively brief life (he died at the age of fifty-five), Descartes warned that "the single design to strip one's self of all past beliefs is one that ought not to be undertaken by everyone." Unless an individual had great self-discipline—like Descartes, presumably—

he would leave the "beaten highway" at his peril, lose himself, "and continue to wander for life."

As the consequence of his own remarkable discoveries, Descartes wrote, he had developed four precepts on the basis of which, he was convinced, all search for knowledge should rest.

> The *first* was never to accept anything for true which I clearly did not know to be such, that is to say, carefully to avoid precipancy and prejudice, and to comprise nothing more in my judgment that what was presented to my mind so clearly and distinctly as to exclude all grounds of doubt.
>
> The *second*, to divide each of the difficulties under examination into as many parts as possible, and as might be necessary for its adequate solution.
>
> The *third*, to conduct my thoughts in such an order that, by commencing with objects the simplest and easiest to know, I might ascend by little and little, and, as it were, step by step, to the knowledge of the more complex, assigning in thought a certain order even to those objects which in their own nature do not stand in a relation of antecedent and sequence.
>
> And last, in every case to make enumerations so complete, and reviews so general, that I might be assured nothing was omitted.

"This Method," Descartes wrote, "from the time I had begun to apply it, had been to me the source of satisfaction so intense as to lead me to believe that more perfect or more innocent could not be enjoyed in this life; and as by this means I daily discovered truths that appeared to me of some importance, and of which other men were generally ignorant, the gratification thence arising so occupied my mind that I was wholly indifferent to every other object."

There is a kind of engaging innocence in Descartes's essay. Having laid down the four essential rules for his Method, he goes on to offer "a provisory code of Morals, composed of three or four maxims. . . . " The first was "to obey the laws and customs of my country, adhering firmly to the Faith [Roman Catholicism] in which, by the grace of God, I had been educated from my childhood." He believed in choosing the most moderate line among different possible courses of action.

A second maxim was to be "firm and resolute" in supporting the conclusions that his studies had led him to consider true and, finally, "to conquer myself rather than fortune, and change my desires rather than the order of the world." Unexceptional precepts on the whole.

The philosophical problem that most troubled Descartes was how to establish the basic building block of reality. He decided it must lie with him. How did he know he existed? It struck him that he knew he existed, not because he was a material body and a particular physiognomy, but because he could think. As he put it, *"I think, hence I am."* The mind was independent of the body and immortal. Everything thus began with the mind. "From the very circumstances that I thought to doubt the truth of other things," Descartes wrote, "it most clearly and certainly followed that . . . I was a substance whose whole essence or nature consists only in thinking," independent of place or "any material thing."

This response provides an interesting contrast to Descartes, for St. Augustine had asked himself the same questions:

> How do I know that I exist? . . . without any delusive representation of images or phantasms, I am most certain that I am, and that I know and delight in this. In respect of these truths, I am not at all afraid of the arguments of the Academicians, who say What if you are deceived? For if I am deceived, I am. For who is not, cannot be deceived; and if I am deceived, by this same token I am. . . . For, as I know that I am, so I know this also, that I know. And when I love these two things, I add to them a certain third thing, namely my love. . . .

If the mind was the ultimate reality in the world and the essence of the person, *Reason* was the instrument by which truth must be revealed. Nothing should be taken on faith: "We ought never to allow ourselves to be persuaded of the truth of anything unless on the evidence of our Reason . . . and not of our imagination or of our senses."

That still left the question for a devout Catholic of the existence of the Deity, a Being that Descartes couldn't observe. Descartes's solution: Since there must be a thing more perfect in the universe than Descartes, that in turn must be God ("There was of necessity some other more perfect Being upon whom I was dependent, and from whom I had received all that I possessed"). Descartes was satisfied that his proof of the existence of God was "at least as certain . . . as any demonstration of Geometry can be." It should be noted that if this disarmingly simple proof of the existence of God satisfied Descartes, it failed signally to satisfy the guardians of Church doctrine, and Descartes, to his bewilderment, soon found himself in disfavor with the Church hierarchy. Mindful of the fate of Galileo, who had been tried as a heretic and forced to recant his announcement of a heliocentric universe, he decided to maintain a discreet silence in order to pursue those studies that he felt he alone could accomplish.

An idea, however bold, cannot expect to make its way in the world until the existing set of ideas that it challenges directly or indirectly has quite exhausted its usefulness and daily demonstrates its inadequacies. What men like Wyclif and Luther had in common with Descartes was a complete disenchantment with the rigid and formal exercises that passed for scholarship under the aegis of the Roman Church. Interestingly enough, both Luther and Descartes were highly critical of the influence of Aristotle in the Church-dominated academies of the seventeenth century. While the protesting reformers of the sixteenth and seventeenth centuries concentrated on the revitalization of Christianity in a spirit that questioned the whole social and political order, Descartes and his successors fixed their attention on the "Sciences" and announced, as we have seen, that Reason was the critical or, in the case of Descartes, the *only* key to unlock the secrets of science. Discovering the Roman Church as a stumbling block, most spectacularly of course in the case of Galileo, they set about to disentangle science and, more generally, philosophy from any connection with the Church. This was done initially by ignoring the Church and subsequently, when the intellectual dissenters felt strong enough, by an all-out attack on the Church—an attack, which at the first instance was directed against the Roman Church and its intellectual agencies, was soon widened to include Christianity in general.

I think it is clear enough that Descartes's *Discourse on Method* had fateful consequences both good and bad. Giving the mind, conceived of as Reason, primacy over every other aspect of the human psyche became the most basic article of faith in the developing religion of man, whose cathedral was to be the modern university. When the religion of man with its faith in scientific "methodology" and devotion to doubting all as the path to knowing all finally took over higher education in the Western world (circa 1890), it left no room for any other form of knowing.

On the more positive side, it must be said that Descartes, along with his allies, men like Galileo and the Englishman Francis Bacon, freed scientific inquiry from the smothering embrace of the Church and launched it on its astonishing career of accomplishment. The bottom-line cost was the alienation of men and women from themselves that is so evident in our world today.

If the seventeenth century was dominated by the Reformation, the eighteenth century was, doubtless in reaction to it, the century of Enlightenment, or, as it was sometimes called, taking its clue from Descartes, the Age of Reason. Primarily, in its initial phase at least, a European phenomenon and a French one at that, it had little impact on colonial America, which from the middle years of the century—from, say, the Stamp Act in 1764 to the end of the Revolutionary War—was preoccupied with its conflict with the mother country. Nevertheless, what the philosophers of the Enlightenment had in mind was nothing less than the complete dismantling of the religion of the city of God—Christianity—and its replacement by the religion of the city of man, a religion of their own devising. Parenthetically, one suspects that the fact that the Enlightenment had its most potent advocates in France, a country predominately Catholic, and where the church was closely allied with a decadent monarchy, was not entirely coincidental.

As Carl Becker has pointed out in *The Heavenly City of the Eighteenth Century Philosophers*, it was necessary to rout Christianity by offering secular substitutes or equivalents for the principal doctrines of the city of God.

Christians, for example, lived in the hope of eternal life in the hereafter, or of a millennium when Christ would return to reign on earth for a thousand years of peace and harmony, and, much more mundanely, and presumably prior to the millennium (although this was not always clear all the time), when men and women would be equal—in Luther's words, "every man a king and priest"—with no one set over another. For the prophets of the Protesting faith, Wyclif, Hus, and Luther prominent among them, that event was to be anticipated in the imaginable future.

For the hope for a life of bliss in the hereafter, the philosophers substituted the prospect of a life of peace and harmony on earth, this to be achieved by Reason and Science, finally freed from the trammels of superstition, that is, religion.

To discredit the role of Christianity in the past, the philosophers wrote history that presented the Church as the cause of most of the miseries and calamities that had beset the species.

For the notion of the Garden of Eden, the philosophers offered the Golden Age of fifth-century Athens.

It was, of course, essential to find a source of authority other than the Deity for those aspects of Christian doctrine that were considered beneficial or "enlightened"; a different and "truer" source. And this, it turned out, was nature.

"Nature" and "natural" thus became the magic, talismanic words. God was nature's backup man. It was even conceded by the Deists that God had started things up. He was the great "Watchmaker" in the sky who had created the watch, ordained the natural laws by which it ran, and then left it to its own "natural" devices. Christianity was not only superfluous, it was an impediment to understanding the TRUTH that was to be found not in a set of doctrines or dogmas but in the very nature of the universe. To understand the world and humankind you went to the world, to nature, which taught all the lessons humanity needed to know. As Becker put it, "Having denatured God, the philosopher deified nature." David Hume, one of the clarion voices of the English Enlightenment, expressed the ruling sentiment of the new religion: Once the philosophers had discovered "the constant and universal principles of human nature," the world could be set right again, as it had been in the time of the Greeks.

In brief: For the Garden of Eden, the philosophers of the French Revolution offered the relatively brief days of high Greek or Athenian culture; for bliss in heaven, they offered bliss on earth; for original sin, they proposed the natural goodness of men and women; for faith, they substituted reason; for Christian teachings, science; for the triune God, nature. Such was the religion of the city of man.

At least one of the philosophers of the Enlightenment, Auguste Comte, the "father of sociology," stated as much. He wished to make sociology "the religion of humanity."

In Becker's words, the philosophers of the Enlightenment

> renounced the authority of the church and Bible
> but exhibited a naive faith in the authority of
> nature and reason. . . . They denied that miracles
> ever happened, but believed in the perfectability
> of the human race. . . . In spite of their ration-
> alism and their humane sympathies, in spite of
> their aversion to hocus-pocus and enthusiasm
> and dim perspectives, in spite of their eager
> skepticism, their engaging cynicism, their brave
> youthful blasphemies and talk of hanging the
> last king in the entrails of the last priest—in spite
> of all of it, there is more of Christian philosophy
> in the writing of the *Philosophes* than has yet
> been dreamt of in our histories.

From the time of Descartes, the French have adored philosophy—philosophy sometimes of a singularly limp
character, philosophy sometimes only slightly elevated
over the philosophy that Goethe ascribed to the dominant
spirit of the eighteenth century where "every one was
now entitled, not only to philosophize, but also by degrees
to consider himself a philosopher. Philosophy, therefore,
was more or less sound and practiced common sense,
which ventured to enter upon the universal, and to decide
upon inner and outer experiences . . . and thus at last Phi-

losophers were found in all the faculties, nay, in all classes and trades.''

By the same token French philosophy has been directed far more to the intellectual and theoretical realm than to the real world. While it is true that the philosophers spun out splendid theories of human freedom and equality and lords and ladies played at being shepherds and shepherd-esses, it was, in the words of the great Viennese historian Egon Friedell, ''a comedy of sentimental brotherhood, with warm words and muzzy emotion, but no one thought to draw from this fine feeling even the most trivial prac-tical result.'' Voltaire's attitude was typical of that of the intellectuals of the Enlightenment and the upper classes generally. Speaking of ''the people,'' he said: ''They will always remain stupid and barbarous; they are oxen who need a yoke, a whip, and hay.''

The new religion had its own deity, the goddess of Reason; its principal prophet was, of course, René Des-cartes. The religion of the city of man, as we have noted, was not satisfied to coexist with the religion of the city of God, it was determined to extirpate the old supersti-tious religion root and branch. It wished to make the two cities, that of God and that of man, one city, thereby vastly simplifying life and transforming the heavenly city of the life hereafter into a here-and-now heaven-on-earth.

One of the few Enlightenment philosophers who came to doubt the primacy, and sufficiency, of Reason was Hume. Hume, in his later years, doubted that Reason was an adequate instrument to cope with any of the basic questions about the meaning of life or the nature of divinity. Having reached that conclusion, he dared not announce it but locked it away in his desk drawer.

7

DECLARATION AND
CONSTITUTION

At this point, we need to consider two classic American documents that have often been taken as examples of Enlightenment thought—the Declaration of Independence and the Federal Constitution.

As we noted, the French Enlightenment, which was to become the dominant version, had little appeal for Americans. There were, after all, three distinct Enlightenments—Scottish, English, and French. The Scottish and English versions, which also exalted reason, did not display the animus toward Christianity that characterized the French variety and were thus far more congenial to Americans. "Reason" had a strong appeal, and, somewhat later, the notion of science as the key to progress.

I have referred elsewhere to the Declaration of Independence as the clarion call of the Secular-Democratic Consciousness, a product of the Enlightenment. On second thought I think it essential to modify this proposition as follows: The Enlightenment, with its determined secularization of the heavenly city and its promise of attaining it on earth through Science and Reason, appropriated the ancient Christian dream of democracy and equality. The Declaration of Independence almost perfectly represents the moment at which those two very distinct traditions, the city of man (which now, for the first time since the primitive church, had its own competing religion) and the city of God, joined forces. On one level the Declaration was simply the latest expression of the Christian democracy and equality proclaimed by the early church, ratified by Augustine in the *City of God* and reasserted in All Souls' Day. It was the lineal descendant of John Wyclif, of Luther and Calvin, of the Levellers and Diggers, and all the radical protesters of the Reformation.

The Virginia Bill of Rights, which was adopted by "a General Convention" held at Williamsburg on the 6th of May, 1776, had a preamble written by Jefferson's mentor, the Virginia lawyer George Mason. It stated that "all men are by nature equally free and independent, and have certain inherent rights, of which, when they enter into a state of society, they cannot by any compact deprive or divest their posterity; namely, the enjoyment of life and liberty, with the means of acquiring and possessing property, and pursuing and obtaining happiness and safety." Mason had adopted, in essence, the Lockean trinity of "life, liberty, and property," adding "happiness" and "safety." Jefferson substituted "happiness" for "property." The reason for Jefferson's omission of "property" is unknown. It is certainly not implausible to conjecture that the reason may have been a deep residual uneasiness about property. From the New Testament to the Declaration of Independence, property had commonly been equated with greed and, in Wyclif and other radical tracterians, with sin.

Another of Jefferson's changes in Mason's preamble was to substitute for the phrase "all men are by nature equally free and independent" the words "are created equal, that they are endowed by *their Creator* [italics mine] with certain inalienable rights. . . ." In other words, where Mason had credited "nature" with the equal condition of men, Jefferson introduced the "Creator." While Jefferson did not say specifically that nature had created men "equally free and independent," he left room for that interpretation, but made it clear that it was "their Creator" who had endowed them with their rights.

When John Quincy Adams delivered his "discourse" before the New York Historical Society on the fiftieth anniversary of the inauguration of George Washington, he had no uncertainty about the "the laws of nature" and "nature's God." "That all men are created *equal*. That to *secure* the rights to life, liberty and the pursuit of happiness, governments are instituted among men, deriving their *just* powers from the *consent* of the governed. All this, is by the laws of nature and of nature's God, and of course presupposes the existence of a God, the moral ruler of the universe, and a rule of right and wrong, of just and unjust, binding upon man, preceding all institutions of human society and government."

The Federal Constitution is the product of the two streams of thought that I have chosen to call Classical-Christian. The classical portion is clear enough. The Founding Fathers had all gone to school with the classical philosophers and historians, especially Polybius, the second-century B.C. historian. The classical world believed that time was cyclical. Events repeated themselves endlessly. The Greeks described three classic ''rotating'' types of government: monarchy, aristocracy, and democracy. Each had a degenerate phase. Monarchy inevitably degenerated into tyranny at which point the aristocracy, indignant at the denial of their rights, would, typically, overthrow the tyrant and rule in the name of the people. In time, the aristocracy would become a corrupt and self-serving oligarchy and thereby become victim of a popular uprising followed by a period of democracy. Since democracy was a notoriously unstable form of government, it could be counted on to slide into anarchy. Since no nation could long endure anarchy, its citizens would turn to a strong leader in the form of a dictator to restore order. Usually, he would seek to legitimate himself by being acclaimed as king or emperor and the cycle would begin once more.

There were two things that were compelling to the generation of the American Revolution about the Greek view of history. The first was simply that Greece and all things Greek had been held in great esteem since the revival of interest in Greece and Rome that began in Italy in the middle of the fifteenth century. The second was that such a view of human frailty and corruptability was entirely congenial with the Christian doctrine of original sin. If, indeed, human beings were rational and reasonable creatures, it was inexplicable how history could be such a record of folly, violence, and irrationality. Not only was there the history of Greece, and of course of Rome as well, to demonstrate the weakness—or wickedness—of the human heart, there was the whole long record in the Old Testament of the bad behavior of the Chosen People, who, despite their covenant (testament) with the Lord, were constantly driving him to the point of distraction by their pursuit of false gods and their lapses into whoredoms and fornications. Nor did the story stop there. There were, as we have seen, the ancient civilizations, the world empires of the Assyrians, Persians, Babylonians, and so on, which had all risen and fallen.

Christianity had, to be sure, straightened out the cycles of the ancients by positing a beginning and an end to history, a story running from creation to the end of time. As we have often had occasion to note, the Christian system, as described most vividly in Augustine, envisioned a constant interaction between the city of man and the city of God with the possibility of an increase in godliness in the city of man by virtue of its direct and immediate involvement with the city of God. So there was an opportunity for a kind of progress, if you will, a process by means of which the devout tried perpetually, or sporadically, to prepare the city of man for the final triumph of the city of God.

Since virtually all of the Founding Fathers were Christians of one denomination or another (Episcopalians constituted the largest single group), they were, each in their own way, believers in the doctrine, however understood, of original sin. That is, they believed that selfishness, greed, and vanity were at least as powerful impulses of the human heart as reason and the desire to do good in the world. It followed from this that, as they frequently observed, it was essential to frame a government that would minimize the opportunities of the rich and powerful to exploit the poor—and, by the same token, to protect the legitimate rights of those with property. That, indeed, was one of the notions behind the idea of checks and balances. According to Montesquieu, government should contain monarchial, aristocratic, and democratic elements. This, it was hoped, would serve to give at least an element of stability and longevity to a government, although it must be said most of the Framers of the Constitutions were not sanguine about the long-range prospects of their handiwork, primarily because of the issue of slavery and secondarily, of course, because the "lesson of history" seemed to be that all human institutions were subject to the ravages of time since they eventually became collecting stations for greed, corruption, and "self-aggrandizement" until they collapsed from the simple weight of their accumulated wickedness. From the perspective of the late eighteenth century, the pattern seemed almost as set to many of the Founders as it had to the ancient Greeks.

There was one other basic assumption that the generation of the Founders shared with their Greek and Roman forebears. Both believed, with certain important differences to be sure, in a system of natural law. There were laws that governed the various aspects of the universe from the Copernican system of the earth revolving around the sun to the simpler laws governing various classes of natural phenomena and, indeed, governing human behavior (although with the Greeks, the gods might intervene capriciously at any time). By the late eighteenth century the prototype of natural law was Newton's majestic Law of Gravity. There were, in addition to the laws of nature, which, like the Law of Gravity, governed the natural world, celestial laws—at least it was so conjectured—which governed the angels in heaven and the souls of men and women made perfect. There was even postulated *lex eterna*, the law by which God governed his own actions, although this was disputed by some theologians since God represented the only complete freedom in the universe. Laws governing human society were generally referred to as municipal laws, and the expectation was that they would be based, so far as possible, on God's intentions for humankind as deduced from Scripture, revelation, and the experience of history.

The notion that there was a system of laws in the universe emboldened the Founders to try the experiment of drafting a constitution that would make possible the governance of this vast new nation. The delegates had, of course, the example of their colonial charters and the experience in New England, at least of the written covenants that the members of individual towns drew up. In addition, by the time the delegates to the Federal Convention met in Washington in the summer of 1787, they had a number of state constitutions to draw on, perhaps most strikingly that of Massachusetts, which John Adams had had a leading role in writing.

The desire, then, to have a "mixed" government, one containing elements of monarchy (a President), aristocracy (the Senate), and democracy (the House), was supplemented by the determination to draft a constitution that, by taking account of "original sin," would minimize the opportunity for one segment of the population to oppress and exploit another. The result, it has often been pointed out, was not a "democracy." In the opinion of the Founders, a democracy was a government in which the will of the people prevailed directly in all cases. Since people in the mass were notoriously volatile, it was essential to place constraints on the direct expression of the popular will. There were other interests or rights that must be protected from some sudden gust of popular passion. The phrase that expressed this best was that the Framers were determined to create "a government of laws not of men." They were careful to call their handiwork a republic.

Much as they knew of history, they believed that it would be a mistake to follow too closely any particular model from the past. In the words of Charles Pinckney, a South Carolina delegate to the Constitutional Convention (1787):

The people of this country are not only very different from the inhabitants of any State we are acquainted with in the modern world but I assert that their situation is distinct from either the peoples of Greece or Rome or any other State we are acquainted with among the ancients. Can the orders introduced by the institution of Solon, can they be found in the United States? Can the military habits & manners of Sparta be reassembled to our habits & manners? Are the distinctions of Patrician & Plebian known among us? Can the Helvitic or Belgic confederacies, or can the unwieldy, unmeaning body called the Germanic Empire, can they be said to possess either the same or a situation like ours? I apprehend not. They are perfectly different, in their distinctions of rank, their Constitutions, their manner & their policy.

The fact was "that after all there is one, but one great & equal body of citizens composing the inhabitants of this Country among whom there are no distinctions of rank, and very few of fortune."

The delegates alluded time after time during the debates to the dangers that could be counted on to beset any republican government. Alexander Hamilton cautioned that the Federal Government must have sufficient power to prevent individual states led by demagogues from constantly contending with it. "The ambition of demagogues

is known to hate the controul of the General Government.
. . . All the passions then we see of avarice, ambition,
interest, which govern most individuals, and all public
bodies, fall into the current of the States. . . . '' It was a
theme Hamilton reverted to repeatedly: ''In every community where industry is encouraged, there will be a
division of it into the few & the many,'' he declared.
''Hence separate interests will arise. There will be debtors
& creditors etc. Give all power to the many, they will
oppress the few. Give all power to the few, they will
oppress the many. Both therefore ought to have the power
to defend itself against the other.''

By balancing the different interests and trying to guard
against the exploitation of one class by another, it was
hoped that the United States would avoid the terrible
disproportions that prevailed in European countries between the incomes of the wealthy and those of the poor.
Pinckney noted that ''the people of the United States are
more equal in their circumstances than the people of any
other Country—that they have very few rich men among
them—by rich men I mean those whose riches may have
a dangerous influence or such as are esteemed rich in
Europe—perhaps there are not one hundred of such upon
the Continent; that it is not probable that this number will
be greatly increased; that the genius of the people, their
mediocrity of situation & the prospects which are afforded
their industry in a Country which must be a new one for
centuries are unfavorable to the rapid distinction of
ranks.''

One of the most conservative members of the Constitutional Convention, Gouverneur Morris of New York, spoke to the same effect:

> The rich [he warned his fellow delegates] will strive to establish their dominion & enslave the rest. They always did. They always will. The proper security against them is to form them into a separate interest. The two forces will then control each other. Let the rich mix with the poor and in a Commercial Country, they will establish an oligarchy. Take away commerce, and the democracy will triumph. Thus it has been all the world over. So it will be among us. Reason tells us that we are but men; and we are not to expect any particular intervention of Heaven in our favor.

Morris expanded on his fear of the rich.

> They will have the same effect here as elsewhere if we do not by such a Government keep them within their proper sphere. We should remember that the people never act from reason alone. The Rich will take advantage of their passions & make these the instruments for oppressing them. . . . The schemes of the Rich will be favored by the extent of the Country. The people in such distant parts can not communicate & act in con-

cert. They will be the dupes of those who have more knowledge & intercourse. The only security against encroachments will be a select & sagacious body of men, instituted to watch against them on all sides.

At the convention, Virginian James Madison, representing the more liberal faction among the delegates, echoed Morris's warning: "All civilized Societies," Madison declared, "would be divided into different Sects, Factions & interests, as they happened to consist of rich & poor, debtors & creditors, the landed, the manufacturing, the commercial interests, the inhabitants of this district or that district, the followers of this political leader or that political leader, the disciples of this religious Sect or that religious Sect. In all cases where a majority are united by a common interest or passion, the rights of the minority are in danger."

Madison expounded the same views—much more discreetly because he was writing for a general audience—in the Tenth Federalist Paper. The paper, as a whole, deals with the problem of factions in a republic, whence does factionalism arise and how it is to be dealt with. In history the "most common and durable source of faction has been the various and unequal distribution of property," Madison wrote. "A landed interest, a manufacturing interest, a merchantile interest, a moneyed interest, with many lesser interests grow up of necessity in civilized nations, and divide them into different classes, actuated by different sentiments and views. The regulation of these various and interfering interests forms the principal task of modern legislation.'' Where certain interests combine, they will exploit the others. As Madison puts it: ''If the impulse and the opportunity be suffered to coincide, we well know that neither moral nor religious motives can be relied on as an adequate control.'' Madison's hope was that the wide geographic range and the variety of conflicting interests would in itself help to prevent such concentrations and combinations as would place the welfare on the larger society at risk. Beyond this, it was the responsibility of government itself to prevent the exploitation of any particular segment of society.

A less famous but more trenchant analysis of American politics than Madison's in terms of original sin was written in 1798 by William Manning, a semiliterate farmer from Billerica, Massachusetts. Manning acknowledges that his view of history is based largely on a series of articles in the *Boston Chronicle* and on his reading of the Bible. The articles, Manning notes, told ''a long & blody history about the fudes & animosityes, contentions & blood sheds that hapned in the antiant Republicks of Athens, Greesh & Roome & many other nations, between the few & Many, the Perthiens, & Plebians, Rich & poor, Dettor & Creditor. . . . '' It was evident to Manning that such distinctions had already appeared in the new republic, and he called on ''all the Republicans, Farmers, Mecanicks, and Labourers'' to join together to protect the interests of the many against exploitation by the few.

"Men are born & grow up in this world with a vast variaty of capacityes, strength & abilityes both of Body & Mind, & have strongly implanted within them numerous pashons & lusts continually urging them to fraud violence & acts of injustis towards one another." Men have at the same time a strong notion of "right and rong" but this understanding wars with a "desire of Selfe Seporte, Selfe Defence, Selfe Love, Selfe Conceit, Selfe Importance, & Selfe agrandisement, that it Ingroses all his care and attention so that he can see nothing beyond Selfe. . . . Give a man honour & he wants more. Give him power & he wants more. Give him money & he wants more. In short he is neaver easy, but the more he has the more he wants."

It was this image of man, so scathingly drawn by Manning, that hovered over the deliberations of the delegates to the Federal Convention. It is ironic that ten years after the adoption of the Constitution, a Massachusetts farmer was accusing the class—"the few"—that had drafted it of showing a disposition to exploit "the many."

The Framers had two major fears concerning the fate of their handiwork. The first was the slavery issue. Much has been made in the present day of the fact that the Framers drafted a document that indirectly at least legitimized slavery and indeed allowed slaves to be counted as property. Slavery certainly was an agonizing issue for the delegates, especially for those from the North, most of whom held strong convictions against slavery. The most impassioned denunciation of slavery was by George Mason, himself a slave-owner. Toward the end of the debates, when the issue of slavery threatened to wreck the convention, Mason spoke out against the continued importation of slaves. "The Western people are already calling out for slaves for their new lands," Mason pointed out, adding:

> Slaves discourage arts & manufactures. The poor despise labor when performed by slaves. They prevent the immigration of Whites, who really enrich & strengthen a Country. They produce the most pernicious effect on manners. Every master of slaves is a petty tyrant. They bring the judgment of heaven on a Country. As nations can not be rewarded or punished in the next world they must be in this. By an inevitable chain of causes & effects providence punishes national sins by national calamities. . . . He held it essential in every point of view that the General Government should have the power to prevent the increase in slavery. . . .

Charles Pinckney of South Carolina spoke for intractable Southerners who would sooner give up the Constitution or sever the precarious confederacy than accept limitations on their "peculiar institution." "If slavery be wrong," Pinckney declared, "it is justified by the example of all the world." He cited the case of "Greece, Rome & other ancient States; the sanction given by France, England, Holland & other modern States." In all ages "one-half of mankind have been slaves." So there you have it. No compromise on the slavery issue, no Constitution. It was a bitter pill for the Northern delegates to swallow. Gouverneur Morris, who had described the slavery dilemma as that of doing "injustice to the Southern States or to Human nature," and had sworn never to put his name to a document that accepted slavery, capitulated. To him the question boiled down to "shall there be a national government or not. . . . " The alternative was "general anarchy."

The question was not one of freeing or not freeing the slaves. If the delegates from the Northern states had been adamant on the slavery issue, the result, as we have seen, would not have been the freeing of the slaves but the division of the confederacy into two separate entities, one slave and one free, with the probable consequence that the slaves would never have been freed.

The second reason that many of the Framers had serious misgivings about the longevity of the Constitution was what we might call the "John Wesley principle" that so concerned the founder of Methodism. The reader may recall that Wesley had a rather fatalistic view of the durability of any Christian reform; "Whenever riches have increased," Wesley wrote, "the essence of religion has decreased in the same proportion. . . . " Many of the Founding Fathers shared Wesley's concern. If true in religion, did it not follow that it must be true in civil society, in the city of man?

Could it not be predicted that a nation enjoying liberty and based on democratic principles would prosper, and would not that prosperity breed luxury, and with luxury would surely come the emergence of a rich and spoiled class, lacking in civic virtue or Christian austerity, and along with a class of self-indulgent rich the concommitant appearance of a deprived and exploited class that would in time rise up in revolutionary rage? Jefferson, who was, for the most part, a prophet of the Enlightenment, believing in the natural goodness of men and women, was so concerned about the probability of this outcome that he wrote a remarkable letter to Madison from Paris, where he was witnessing the horrors of the French Revolution, proposing that privately held property be redistributed every generation so that it could not accumulate in the hands of a few great property owners.

Many of the Founders, John Adams among them, brooding about the "luxury problem," felt that even with all the Constitution's built-in safeguards designed to mitigate the abuse of power, its ultimate success must rest on the character of the people. If the people *en masse* became greedy and selfish, lacking in vigilance, then the republic must come tumbling down in decadence and decay. "Our constitution was written for a moral and religious people," Adams wrote, "and it is wholly inadequate for the government of any other."

Still and all, the beginnings of the new government were accompanied, in the main, by a general euphoria. Such gloomy speculations as those of John Adams were the exception. Most Americans believed the words on the Great Seal of the United States taken from Virgil's *Aeneid*: "A New Age [or series of Ages] Now Begins." It was not simply a new age for Americans but a new age for humanity. This was the "radical universalism" of the Revolution, as the English critic Wyndham Lewis called it.

On July 4, 1786, the Reverend Samuel Thacher gave a sermon at Concord, Massachusetts. His theme was that liberty was "a pure, original emanation from the great source of Life." It had been almost obliterated from the earth "when AMERICA, indignant at oppression, rose and proclaimed it with a voice which broke the spell of the confining nations . . . and struck like thunder on the ears of despots." Arbitrary government, oppression, and exploitation must give way all over the earth to the determination of peoples to be free and equal. "All hail! Approaching Revolutions!" Thacher exclaimed. "Americans, we have lived ages in a day. Pyramids of lawless power, the work of centuries, have fallen in a moment!" The effects of the revolution "are not confined to one age or one country." Its influence would be extended "beyond calculation," marking "the subsequent emancipation of a world."

The "radical universalism" of the revolutionary generation was underlined by histories written in the decades following the Revolution. Several of them were entitled *Universal History*, viz. David Ramsay's *Universal History or An Historical View of Asia, Africa, Europe and America from Their Earliest Records to the Nineteenth Century with Particular Reference to the State of Society, Literature, Religion, and Form of Government in the United States of America.*

When Frederick Butler published his *Complete History of the United States of America, Embracing the Whole Period from the Discovery of North America down to the Year 1820*, he noted in his preface that, in order to grasp fully the significance of the history of the United States, it was "necessary to trace the history of the family of man, from the creation to the flood, and from the flood down to the present time, and [show] the special government of God." Butler declared that the "principles of civil and religious liberty, which formed the basis of the wise and virtuous institutions of our fathers, and laid the foundations of the United States of America, originated in the Puritan Church, and were unknown to any former age of the world, and have never been enjoyed by any other people, either before or since, and probably never will be until the millennial day."

A comparison between the American and French revolutions is instructive. The motto of the French Revolution was "Liberté, Egalité, Fraternité." There was little of any of those elements. Carl Becker, in his *Heavenly City of the Eighteenth Century*, evokes the moment when "Citizen Robespierre, with a bouquet in one hand and a torch in the other, inaugurated the new religion of humanity by lighting the conflagration that was to purge the world of ignorance, vice, and folly.'' Robespierre was the word of Voltaire made flesh.

The French Revolution was the first revolution based on the new religion of man: the religion of Science and Reason. Appropriating the Christian ideal of democracy and equality, it was aggressively hostile to Christianity itself, or, more specifically, to the Roman Church, which was closely allied with the nobility. In an orgy of violence, the French peasants, oppressed for centuries, murdered not only their lords but thousands of monks and nuns who were associated in the popular mind with their oppressors. The god of the religion of man was, as we have noted, a goddess, to whom altars were raised about the land while the guillotine proved insatiable. When the available aristocrats had been consumed by that hideous blade, it began to fall on the necks of the more moderate revolutionaries, devouring, as it was said, its own children, meanwhile proclaiming the perfectability of man and the imminence of the heavenly city on earth. Of course, if, in a terrible lust of idealism, it was necessary to murder many thousands of individuals who, however free and equal theoretically, held to the wrong ideas, that was, as the next two centuries would demonstrate, a small price to pay for establishing heaven on earth.

Killing people who held the wrong ideas was not, of course, a wholly new development in the history of the human race. The adherents of the Roman and of the

Protesting churches had been up to it quite recently. What was new was the notion that such bloody acts were to be undertaken in the name of the goddess of Reason and under the banner of Science. What was more remarkable still was that the French Revolution, which had been undertaken in the name of the rights of men and women of every nation, should have been such a hit in the new United States. This was doubtlessly due at least in part to the fact that both the American and French Revolution had proclaimed their revolutions on behalf of the liberation of the oppressed of every land.

Thus, it was not surprising that the French Revolution appeared to many Americans to be simply a splendid extension of their own. There was even a kind of proprietary feeling in the United States, as if the French Revolution were the somewhat ill-favored offspring of its American predecessor. Enthusiastic American supporters of the French Revolution wore French tricolor cockades in their hats, sang the "Marsailles," and sported miniature guillotines. Even more oddly, Americans discovered an affinity for many of the ideas of the Enlightenment. The third President of the United States, Thomas Jefferson, was the principal American proponent of the Enlightenment. He even undertook to rewrite the New Testament to make it more compatible with the enlightened thought of the age and he chided John Adams for thinking that the most important task in education was to pass on the accumulated wisdom of the past. Surely Adams had been misquoted. He had "too much science" himself not to know that the main purpose of education was to convey to the student the latest scientific information, not the musty records of bygone days.

The French Revolution stepped forward to claim to speak in an enlightened voice for the emancipation of humankind. It thus, in effect, appropriated the American Revolution, stripped it of its ecclesiastical elements, and proclaimed to the world the new religion of man. Americans bought the religion of man and found the notion of progress through Science and Reason irresistible. They liked the idea that human beings were naturally good, reasonable creatures, and they believed devoutly that the United States was the chosen vessel of the Lord. Nor were they apparently troubled by the fact that most of them, at the same time that they embraced the religion of man, clung fast to the principal, if contradictory, tenets of the Christian faith. Multitudes of them went dutifully to church on Sundays (and often on other days as well), prayed, recited one Christian creed or another, and saw no contradiction between their "civil religion" and their professed Christian faith.

8

RADICAL PROTESTANTISM IN NINETEENTH-CENTURY AMERICA

Even among those critics of Max Weber, who have rejected his notion that "Puritanism" was hospitable to capitalism, there has been a clear disposition to assume that once capitalism had raised its head, ugly or otherwise, Protestantism made the necessary accommodations and subsequently played an inconsiderable role in the perpetual struggle for social justice. This attitude is primarily the result of an inclination to concentrate on the institutional life of Protestant Christianity in the United States, which is to say, specifically, on the history of the major denominations.

To do so is to seriously underestimate the role of radical Christians operating independently of organized religion—and often in direct opposition to it. Throughout the nineteenth and well into the twentieth century, radical Protestantism affected every area of American life and led the fight to mitigate the cruelest injustices of a rapacious capitalism.

Alexis de Tocqueville is generally conceded to have been the most perceptive observer of American life and mores in the nineteenth century. Tocqueville came to the United States in 1830 with a friend to study the American penal system, which he decided was pretty dreadful, but he became fascinated with the nature and the prospects of the world's first modern democracy and with the obsession of Americans with equality. In his preface to *Democracy in America*, Tocqueville states his mission: "The organization and the establishment of democracy in Christendom is the great political problem of our times. The Americans unquestionably have not solved this problem, but they furnish useful data to those who undertake to resolve it." Tocqueville considered the United States a kind of experimental political laboratory for the rest of the world. In his view the remarkable freedom that Americans enjoyed was the direct result of Protestant Christianity. "It never instructs the Americans more fully in the art of being free than when it says nothing of freedom . . . ," he wrote. It seemed to Tocqueville that by contrast in France "the spirit of religion and the spirit of freedom" were always "marching in the opposite directions." In America the case was quite different. "On my arrival in the United States," he wrote, "the religious aspect of the country was the first thing that struck my attention; and the longer I stayed there, the more I perceived the great political consequences resulting from this new state of things.''

While it was true that religion in the United States was fragmented into numerous sects, at the same time there was ''no country in the world where the Christian religion retain[ed] a greater hold over the souls of men than in America. . . . Religion in America takes no direct part in the government of the country, but it must be regarded as the first of their political institutions, for if it does not impart a taste for freedom, it facilitates the use of it. . . . The Americans combine the notions of Christianity and of liberty so intimately in their minds that it is impossible to make them conceive the one without the other. . . . '' Moreover, it seemed clear to Tocqueville, as it had to John Adams and, indeed, most of the Founding Fathers, that Christianity was an essential element in a democracy, far more so than in a monarchy. ''How is it possible,'' Tocqueville asked, ''that society should escape destruction if the moral tie is not strengthened in proportion as the political tie is relaxed? And what can be done with a people who are their own masters if they are not submissive to the Deity?''

Related directly to the passion for liberty was the obsession of Americans with equality. ''Among the novel objects that attracted my attention during my stay in the United States,'' Tocqueville wrote, ''nothing struck me more forcibly than the general equality of condition among the people. I readily discovered the prodigious influence that this primary fact exercises on the whole course of society. . . . The more I advanced in the study of American society, the more I perceived that the equality of condition is the fundamental fact from which all others seem derived." It was evident to the whole world "that a great democratic revolution is going on among us. . . . The whole book [*Democracy in America*]," he added, "that is here offered to the public has been written under a kind of religious awe produced in the author's mind by the view of that irresistible revolution which has advanced for centuries in spite of every obstacle. . . . " The rise of democracy in America seemed to Tocqueville clear evidence of God's power in the world. The "gradual and progressive development of social equality" was "at once the past and future" of the history of the race, and "this discovery alone would confer upon the change the sacred character of a divine decree. To attempt to check democracy would be . . . to resist the will of God."

In America, democracy had been abandoned to "its wild instincts" and it had "grown up like those children who had no parental guidance." What was needed was "a new science of politics for a new world." And it was this "new science" that so preoccupied Tocqueville. There was only one country in the world "where the great social revolution that I am speaking of seems to have reached its natural limits. It has been effected with ease and simplicity; say rather that this country is reaping the fruits of the democratic revolution which we [France] are undergoing without having had the revolution itself.'' ''I confess,'' Tocqueville wrote, ''that in America I saw more than America; I sought there the image of democracy itself, with its inclinations, its character, its prejudices, and its passions, in order to learn what we have to fear or to hope from its progress.''

While industry in the United States was still in its infancy compared with Europe, what Tocqueville saw of the American ''manufacturing aristocracy'' in the early 1830s convinced him that it was ''one of the harshest that ever existed in the world.'' At the moment it seemed also one of the ''most confined and least dangerous. Nevertheless,'' he added, ''the friends of democracy should keep their eyes fixed in this direction; for if ever a permanent inequality of conditions and aristocracy again penetrates into the world, it may be predicted that this is the gate by which they will enter.''

Tocqueville's principal concern, like that of many of the Founders, was that a successful democracy would bring with it prosperity and with prosperity an undue emphasis on material things. An understandable desire for comfort and well-being would thus grow eventually into a ''restless searching for physical gratification,'' a term the Founding Fathers called ''luxury.'' How this increasing preoccupation with ''material objects'' could be moderated or contained was not clear to Tocqueville. As he put it: ''If it be easy to see that it is more particularly important in democratic ages that spiritual opinions should prevail, it is not easy to say by what means those who govern democratic nations may make them predominate."

Tocqueville was not, of course, the only foreign visitor to comment on the centrality of religion in the lives of the great majority of Americans. Moritz Busch, a German journalist who came to the United States with the idea of settling here, wrote: "Not since the fire of the Reformation was extinguished by dogmatism has the religious spirit expressed itself in any part of the Christian world as powerfully as among the people of the United States—and in no place so chaotically and strangely." Compared to Germany, "the life of the Christian Church in America seems almost like a remnant of the fantastically fluid primeval world alongside the solid regularity and rational dryness of present-day nature. . . . Beneath the crust of a rigid and obstinate orthodoxy . . . has boiled since the arrival of the first Puritan ship on Plymouth's shores, and still boils and flows today, a volcanic wonder-fire. At times it runs through the land in the form of will-o'-the-wisps, so that rational people, confused, shake their heads about it, and at other times it flares up in intense revivals." A new movement, "having ignited the minds of the masses with its fervor . . . deposits as slag the constitution of a new sect. The spirit which once descended upon the disciples in flaming tongues is still dispersed here in abundance, and every year thousands do not merely celebrate but actually experience Pentecost."

If the character of the nation was, as Tocqueville believed, determined by the religious convictions of its citizens, it was also true that the quality of American life was subject to severe criticism from Christian reformers who, from the earliest days of the republic, saw much that cried out for correction. Initially, the attention of the reform-minded fixed on the issue of drunkenness. Intemperance, as it was more tactfully called, had been a problem since the earliest days of settlement. On the eve of the American Revolution, John Adams deplored the number of taverns (twelve) in the little town of Braintree, Massachusetts. In them, he wrote, "the time, the money, the health, and the modesty, of most of the young and many of the old, are wasted; here diseases, vicious habits, bastards, and legislators, are frequently begotten." Intemperance was the curse of the country in Adams's opinion. In any event, drunkenness was sufficiently widespread to constitute a public scandal in the new republic. The consequence was that the temperance movement was the first great reform efforts of Christian men and women. Susan B. Anthony made a name for herself as a temperance lecturer; Abraham Lincoln was another popular temperance lecturer.

In the first great crusade against the "spirituous liquors," several states, Maine prominent among them, passed laws prohibiting the sale or consumption of alcohol, which were later repealed. The temperance crusaders were convinced that intemperance was the principal— slavery excepted—defect that stood between the states and the realization of the dream of a perfected Union. The significance of the temperance movement was that a cadre of middle-class Christian reformers emerged who carried on two vastly more successful crusades: first, for the rights of women and, more important, the antislavery/abolition crusade.

Although the word *capitalist* nowhere appears in the writings of the Founding Fathers, they, as we have noted, were uneasy about the tendency in societies for wealth to accumulate in the hands of ''the few'' at the cost of ''the many,'' and for luxury to undermine the moral fiber of a people, leading inevitably to their degeneration and downfall. They clearly considered ''commercial liberty'' an important aspect of that larger liberty guaranteed to all (slaves aside). If capitalism was not in the vocabulary of the Founders, it soon manifested itself in the real world. Banks were the essence of capitalism; no banks, no capital and hence no capitalism. But an essentially agricultural people feared and distrusted banks and bankers. It was one of the relatively few things John Adams and his friend Thomas Jefferson agreed upon—the perniciousness of banks and bankers. The trouble with banks was that they made money with other people's money. They did not turn out a reliable, useful item like a horseshoe or a wagon or a spade. But Americans, it turned out, were determined to have capital, initially and most spectacularly, to build canals and almost equally to speculate in land. Innumerable stock companies were formed, investors recruited, and canals built all up and down the country from Virginia north to Vermont. The great majority of them lost money, very substantial sums of money. Banks founded on optimism and illusion failed with monotonous regularity.

The first substantial industries in the new republic were the cotton mills of Lowell and Lawrence in Massachusetts—mills operated by bright young farm girls who formed literary societies and published their poems and essays. It was all the wonder of the world and, as it turned out, as ephemeral as the life of the fruit fly. Soon the darker face of industrialism was everywhere evident.

A severe depression in 1817 gave a jolt to the innate optimism of Americans and caused great hardship among the numerous unemployed. When a soup kitchen opened in New York City, it fed 1,200 persons in the first twenty-four hours, and in a few weeks the number swelled to 6,640. In Philadelphia, one kitchen gave out 24,000 quarts of soup in a few months. Robberies became commonplace and gangs of unemployed youths roamed the streets of the major cities. Working men and women suffered the most from the state of the economy. In Philadelphia, in 1822, millwrights and machine workers of that city met and passed resolutions calling for a limit of the workday from 6:00 A.M. until 6:00 P.M. with an hour for breakfast and dinner, and efforts to form unions were widespread and as widely resisted. What came to be called "the war between capital and labor" was in its infancy, but labor found its champions among the Christian reformers.

As early as the 1830s, William Ellery Channing, a Congregational minister, formed the Christian Union to press for some form of Christian socialism. Four years later he joined with other reformers to found the Religious Union of Associationists. In the first issue of the group's magazine, *The Present*, Channing described their purpose: to redeem the American people who had "allowed the excessive development of the animal passions, exaggerated the element of self; confused the judgments, weakened the power of the spiritual faculties; broken true society; in various degrees became incapable of receiving life from heaven; and so interrupted the divine order, and introduced depraved social tendencies, diseases, and natural confusions, which react to multiply evils." Americans had brought such evils on themselves by "our savage robberies of the Indians, our cruel and wanton oppressions of the Africans, our unjust habits of white serfdom [a reference to the conditions of free labor], our grasping national ambition, our eagerness for wealth, our deceitful modes of external and internal trade, our jealous competitions between different professions and callings, our aping of aristocratic distinctions, our licentiousness and sensuality, our profligate expenditures, public and private." Only when Americans had reformed and sought forgiveness would the nation be summoned "to prove the reality of human brotherhood."

An even bolder critic of the prevailing order was Orestes Brownson. In 1836, Brownson founded the Society for Christian Union and Progress and spelled out his views that same year in *New Views of Christianity, Society and the Church*. In an essay on "The Laboring Classes," which appeared in 1840, Brownson declared: "No one can observe the signs of the times with much care, without perceiving that a crisis as to the relation of wealth and labor is approaching." The old war between kings and barons was over and a new war was under way, a war between "wealth and labor." After a vivid description of the conditions of labor, Brownson characterized the average employer as one who would "fain pass for a Christian and a republican. He shouts for liberty, stickles for equality, and is horrified at a Southern planter who keeps slaves. . . . Wages is a cunning device of the devil, for the benefit of tender consciences, who would retain all the advantages of the slave system, without the expense, trouble and odium of being slave-holders. . . . Our business is to emancipate the proletaries. . . . This is our work. There must be no class of our fellow men doomed to toil through life as mere workmen at wages."

Banks were the principal enemy in Brownson's view. Following the destruction of the banks "must come that of all monopolies, of all PRIVILEDGE." Property was "the root of all the evil that bedeviled the society." It should only last as long as the lifetime of its owner. "Democracy," Brownson wrote, "is based on the fundamental truth that there is an element of the supernatural in every man placing him in relation with universal and absolute truth. . . . Democracy rests, therefore, on spiritualism, and is of necessity a believer in God and in Christ. Nothing but spiritualism has the requisite unity and universality to meet the needs of the masses."

Brownson is an interesting case for another reason. To the astonishment and dismay of his friends he became a convert to the Roman Church. His reasons were that he had lost faith in the ability of Protestant Christianity to achieve the social reforms that he believed essential; that he had come to reject the excessive individualism of Protestantism, and found peace and joy in the Catholic sense of community. In Protestant Christianity everything was sustained by the individual will; that was in time exhausting.

The Reverend Theodore Parker, a Congregational minister, became in the 1830s one of the spokesmen for the new religion of Transcendentalism. "Christianity," he declared, "is a simple thing, very simple. It is absolute, pure morality; absolute pure religion; the love of man; the love of God acting without let or hinderance. . . . Its watchword is: Be perfect as your Father in heaven. The only form it demands is divine life; doing the best thing, in the best way, from the highest motives." The existing sects and denominations would wither away, Parker predicted, and some "new form will take its place. . . . " "The Divine, whether Him or Her [Parker often spoke of God as Mother] was single, a Being of infinite perfection."

Americans, Parker insisted, "do not know how sick we are." Most dismal of all was slavery. "Every seventh man is property." In addition, there was the state of women, who nowhere had her "natural right," who was imprisoned in loveless marriages "worse than celibacy."

To Parker it was clear that there were two classes in America, "the victims of society and the foes of society; the men that organize its sins, and then tell us that nobody is to blame."

The overriding sin, of course, was slavery. It was the clearest and most dramatic case of the strained relationship between the city of God and the city of man. The enslavement of Africans ran counter to all the enlightened opinion of the age, Christian or secular. Yet it was clear that the city of man was prepared to condone it, alien as it was to its tenets concerning the rights of man.

The enormous task of freeing the slaves thus fell to the dwellers of the city of God. The vast majority of abolitionists were radical Protestants. William Jay, son of John Jay, the first chief justice of the Supreme Court, a pacifist, an opponent of the Mexican War, and a leading abolitionist, wrote: "I do not depend on anyone as an abolitionist who does not act from a sense of religious obligation."

The experience of Richard Henry Dana, the author of *Two Years Before the Mast*, a graduate of Harvard, a prominent Boston lawyer, and the scion of one of New England's great families, is instructive. His first visit to an antislavery convention did not impress him. "Nothing," he wrote in his diary, "can exceed the wildness & fanaticism of that collection of people. . . . Two or three women . . . spoke, but their speeches were painful from the sense they gave one of incoherence & excitement amounting almost to insanity. . . . The elements of which this convention was composed,'' Dana added, ''are dreadful. Heated, narrow minded, self willed, excited, un-Christian, radical energies set to work upon a cause which is good, if rightly managed. . . . They are nearly at the extreme of radicalism, socialism & infidelity.'' Yet a few years later, Dana was defending runaway slaves from their pursuers and was himself denounced, ridiculed, and cut dead on the streets of Boston by old friends.

When the principal Christian denominations equivocated on the slavery issue, the abolitionists waved them aside like a mere impediment. Angelina Grimké, the famous South Carolina abolitionist, called on all ''lay Christians,'' men and women alike, to go out and ''declare the *whole* counsel of God to the people. The whole Church Government must come down, the clergy stand in the way of reform, and I do not know but what this stumbling block too must be removed *before* slavery can be abolished, for the system is supported by *them*.''

The third annual report of the New England Anti-Slavery Society defined what was meant by immediate abolition. ''It means, in the first place, that all title of property in the slaves shall instantly cease, because their Creator has never relinquished his claim of ownership, and because none have a right to sell their bodies or buy those of their own species as cattle. . . . Abolish slavery,'' the report read, ''and the gospel will have free course, run, and be glorified; salvation will flow in a current broad and deep. . . . In fine, immediate abolition would save the lives of the planters, enhance the value of their lands, promote the temporal and eternal interests and secure for them the benignant smiles of heaven.''

When the American Anti-Slavery Society was formed, primarily by abolitionists from New York and Boston, the poet John Greenleaf Whittier helped to draft its Declaration of Sentiments. (American temperance campaigner Frances Willard called Whittier ''the household poet of our abolition family. We knew more of him by heart, in all senses of that phrase, than any other singer living or dead.'')

The Declaration eschewed the use of violence. Its intention was to destroy ''error by the potency of truth—the overthrow of prejudice by the power of love—and the abolition of slavery by the spirit of repentance.'' At the same time it declared defiantly that ''all those laws which are now in force, admitting the right of slavery, are . . . before God utterly null and void; being an audacious usurpation of the Divine prerogative, a daring infringement of the law of nature, a base overthrow of the very foundations of the social compact.'' The relationship between the federal government and the slave states was ''criminal and full of danger, and MUST BE BROKEN UP.'' The trust of the abolitionists was ''solely in GOD. *We* may be personally defeated, but our principles never, TRUTH, JUSTICE, REASON, HUMANITY, must and will gloriously triumph . . . whether we live to witness the triumph . . . or perish untimely as martyrs in this great, benevolent and holy cause.'' The delegates then resolved that ''with entire confidence in the overruling justice of

God, we plant ourselves upon the Declaration of Independence and the truths of divine revelation. . . . We shall organize anti-slavery societies, if possible, in every city, town and village in the land. We shall send forth agents to lift up the voice of remonstrance, of warning, of entreaty and rebuke. We shall circulate unsparingly and extensively anti-slavery tracts and periodicals.'' And so they did. Between thirty and forty journals and newspapers carried the anti-slavery message. Besides the *Liberator*, the most prominent were the *National Anti-Slavery Standard*, the *Philanthropist*, the *Anti-Slavery Bugle*, the *Herald of Freedom*, the *Emancipator*, and the *National Era*. The *Slaves' Friend* was directed at children. In addition, a veritable flood of antislavery books poured from Northern presses, many of them the narratives of escaped slaves.

The famous poets of the day, Whittier, most notably, but William Cullen Bryant and Henry Wadsworth Longfellow as well, wrote antislavery poems. James Russell Lowell wrote ''Stanzas on Freedom.''

> Men: whose boast it is that ye
> Come of father brave and free,
> If there breathe on earth a slave,
> Are you truly free and brave?
> If ye do not feel the chain,
> When it works a brother's pain,
> Are ye not base slaves indeed,
> Slaves unworthy to be freed.

Arrested, beaten, stoned, their meeting places burned down around them, abused and reviled (one abolitionist, John Rankin, estimated he had been "mobbed" more than a hundred times), the abolitionists persevered. From a despised handful, they became a mighty army of the Lord and finally touched the conscience of a nation that called itself Christian.

And so it came about that the city of God indeed triumphed over the city of man: Slavery was abolished. As surely as we can say anything about our past, we can say radical Protestants freed the slaves. The religion of the city of man could never have brought about the emancipation of the slaves. The fact was that all the "objective" evidence, the evidence of the senses, the empirical evidence, was that slaves were "inferior" to whites. Soon Darwinism would appear to confirm what the senses testified to—Africans were, according to this new school, a simpler, earlier form of human being on the evolutionary scale. Not inferior, necessarily, but "lower," more rudimentary. Since the religion of the city of man had accepted the Christian doctrines of equality and freedom, it (the religion of man) deplored slavery, but deplored it more in the abstract and showed no inclination to man the barricades in opposition to it, or to join forces with the abolitionists in their crusade. Against the heavily prevailing social sentiment, the abolitionists had only the Scriptural assurance that God made "of one blood all the nations of the earth," that he loved all his creatures equally; no, that he loved the poor, the suffering, and the oppressed *more* than the rich and powerful. The black slave was the living symbol of Christ, the "suffering servant." The equality of the black slave, indeed, in certain essential ways, the *superiority* of the black slave, was quite literally an article of faith for many abolitionists. Had not Christ said that the last should be first?

The inability of "science" to deal with the racial issue was clearly demonstrated at the end of the century when science had established its unquestioned hegemony over the universities and over American intellectual life generally. The two "social sciences" most directly concerned with the racial issue—sociology and anthropology—both under the spell of Darwinism, asserted not only the inferiority of blacks but of non-Anglo-Saxons in general, including specifically the vast numbers of immigrants crowding into the United States from Central Europe. "Racism," born in the darker recesses of the human heart, was initially confirmed by "science."

9

POPULISTS AND SOCIALISTS

In the aftermath of the Civil War, a mood of skepticism became evident in the country. Relatively immune to the currents of the Enlightenment that had so influenced European intellectual circles (and which Max Weber had called "the disenchantment of the world"), American intellectuals now felt the lure of the religion of man: the promise of Science and Reason to be the avatars of progress. Henry Adams described the phenomenon with poignance unusual for him.

To Adams, this loss of faith in traditional religion "was the strangest event of his adult life." He confessed to an "aching consciousness of a religious void" and wondered whether "any large faction of society cared for a future life, or even for the present one. . . . Not an act, or expression, or an image, showed depth of faith or hope. . . . Of all the conditions of his youth which afterwards puzzled the grown-up man, this disappearance of religion puzzled him most." "That the most powerful emotion, next to the sexual, should disappear," Adams added, "might be a personal defect of his own; but that the most intelligent society, led by the most intelligent clergy, in the most moral conditions that he ever knew, should have solved all the problems of the universe so thoroughly as to have quite ceased making itself anxious about past or future . . . seemed to him the most curious phenomenon he had to account for in a long life."

His brother, Charles Francis Adams, Jr., lost his faith about the same time. In 1865, the younger Adams "chanced upon a copy of John Stuart Mill's essay on August Comte," as he reported in his autobiography, " . . . and that essay of Mills revolutionized in a single morning my whole mental attitude. I emerged from the theological stage, in which I had been nurtured, and passed into the scientific. I had up to that time never heard of Darwin. . . . From reading that compact little volume of Mills' . . . I date a changed intellectual and moral being."

The new religion, as Charles Francis Adams's comments suggest, was Darwinism. At the moment when the ideas of the Enlightenment were losing a good deal of their original charm, Charles Darwin (or rather the doctrine of Social Darwinism propounded in his name by the philosopher Herbert Spencer) gave the religion of man a rejuvenating shot in the arm.

A prodigious producer, Spencer published *Principles of Psychology* in 1853. In 1876, the third volume of *Principles of Sociology* appeared. It undertook to apply

Darwinian principles to all human experience, and was doubtless an inspiration for the National Liberal Reform League of which Lester Ward, the "father" of American sociology, was one of the founders. The League was pledged to all in its power to undermine "the leading doctrinal teachings of the so-called Catholic and Evangelical Protestant Churches" and thereby ensure "the triumph of reason and science over faith and theology."

The Darwinian notion of the survival of the fittest had great charm for capitalists who, by becoming capitalists, had demonstrated that they were "the fittest." Competition, it turned out, was the basic fact of animal and human existence: most important of all, the vector of that magic word, progress. Cooperation was for sissies, those not tough enough or ruthless enough to "win" in the merciless contest of life. Charles Sanders Peirce, perhaps our greatest philosopher, entered a dissenting opinion:

> [It] has been strongly maintained and is to-day widely believed that all acts of charity and benevolence, private and public, go seriously to degrade the human race. . . . Here then is the issue. The Gospel of Christ says that progress comes from every individual merging his individuality in sympathy with his neighbors. On the other hand the conviction of the nineteenth century is that progress takes place by virtue of every individual striving for himself with all his might and trampling his neighbor under foot

whenever he gets a chance to do so. This may
accurately be called the Gospel of Greed.

If Charles Francis Adams was beguiled by the new religion of Darwinism, his brother Henry was scornful. He
considered Darwinism "absurdly unscientific." "Unbro-
ken Evolution under uniform conditions," Adams wrote,
"pleased everyone except curates and bishops; it was the
very best substitute for religion; a safe, conservative,
practical, thoroughly Common-Law deity. . . . The idea
was seductive in its perfection; and it had the charm of
art. . . . In geology as in theology," it could only be
proved that "Evolution . . . did not evolve; Uniformity
was not uniform; and Selection did not select." To or-
thodox Darwinians, though not to Darwin himself, "Natural Selection seemed to be a dogma to be put in place
of the Athanasian Creed; it was a form of religious hope;
a promise of ultimate perfection." Since it was all the
rage, Adams declared himself "a Darwinian for fun."

The so-called war between science and religion, the
title of a book by Andrew White, president of Cornell
University, published in 1896, was relatively brief. The
religion of man, the Enlightenment religion of Reason
and Science, now reinforced by Darwinism, drove the
religion of the city of God from the great citadels of
learning, the grand new post–Civil War universities, private and public. In the words of John Jay Chapman,
"Science after Darwin's time was seized with a fever of
world conquest; its language must dominate. In correct

circles it became bad form to use any words that were tinged with theology. New words were invented; modern psychology was developed. . . . The word 'God' was, of course, taboo, unfair, incorrect, a boorish survival.'' Religion was an illusion; ''methods of accurate research had recorded a zero.'' The truth was to be discovered by the application of the appropriate ''methodology.'' Descartes would have been charmed.

But that, of course, was only half the story. With the slaves freed to face a future as arduous in some ways as slavery itself, the attention of those Protestants whose passion it was to redeem the world, starting with the United States, took up the cause of the industrial workers. From the end of the Civil War to the 1920s, the war between Capital and Labor—far bloodier and more protracted than the war between science and religion—occupied the attention of the country. The severe depression of 1876, coming as it did on the centennial of the American Revolution, was a reminder of how rickety the American economy was, having logged depressions as bad or worse in 1817, 1837, and 1854. The depression of 1876 triggered the Great Strikes that shut down much of the nation's railroad system for weeks and exploded in wild riots in Baltimore, New York, Chicago, and a number of towns and cities.

One of the foremost critics of post–Civil War capitalism was Lyman Abbott, Henry Ward Beecher's successor as pastor at the Plymouth Congregational Church. Abbott acknowledged that capitalism had achieved remarkable results. It had been the sponsor of "invention and discovery, and made the unnumbered improvements on which modern life is based: but these accomplishments had been shadowed by the tendency of capitalism to concentrate power in the hands of a few unscrupulous men, widen the gap between the classes, oppress its workers and encourage competition rather than cooperation." What was urgently needed was "the application of new principles to industrial life. . . . For all the good that competition has wrought," Abbott declared, "the principle is now a destructive one." In 1887, Abbott joined with Henry Codman Potter, the Episcopal bishop of New York, to found the Church Association for the Advancement of the Interests of Labor. Its monthly journal, the *Hammer and Pen*, was plainly socialist in tone.

Washington Gladden, a Congregational minister, preached what he called "applied Christianity," and came down firmly on the side of labor. "The present state of the industrial world," he wrote, "is a state of war." Gladden and a number of other advocates of the Social Gospel argued that sin, which had been regarded as a purely personal matter, had, under capitalism, become institutionalized. The sin was not so much in individuals, although there was plenty of that, but in the "systems," the great institutional structures that dominated American life. And most clearly sin was in unrestrained and undomesticated capitalism, which claimed the world. As early as 1874, Horace Bushnell, a Congregational minister, had made the same point. "Evil, once beginning to exist, inevitably becomes organic and constructs a kind of principate or kingdom opposite to God. . . . Corrupt opinions, false judgments, bad manners, and a general body of conventionalism that represent the motherhood of sin, come into vogue and reign, and so, doubtless, everywhere and in all the worlds, sin had it in its nature to organize, mount into the ascendant above God and truth and reign in a kingdom opposite to God." This, in fact, was the condition of so-called American capitalism: "it wished to usurp God's kingdom and have no measure of its conscience but that of its own devising." The real task of Christianity was therefore not the defense of Christian orthodoxy against the assaults of skeptics and free-thinkers, but the extension of the teachings of Christianity ever wider into the world. "The world," Bushnell wrote, "is still too coarse, too deep in sense and in the force-principle, to feel, in any but a small degree, the moral power of God in the Christian history."

Of the evangelists of Christian socialism, George Herron was the most notable. A sociology professor at Iowa College (later Grinnell), he began preaching "Christian Socialism" to his classes, which soon became so popular that he had to move to the college chapel. In 1890, his address to a gathering of Congregationalists on "The Message of Jesus to Men of Wealth" brought him instant notoriety. To Herron, the message of Christianity was sacrifice—"the sacrifice of Christ upon the cross as the unquenchable call of all Christians to sacrifice." America had indeed been anointed by the Lord to be a light to all nations but it had reaped desolation instead. "We have betrayed our trust," Herron declared, "and forsaken our mission. God is disappointed in this nation. We are a fallen nation, an apostate people. . . . We have used the liberty wherewith [our fathers] sacrifice made us free, to rob and oppress one another. . . . The nation is sick at heart, and the body politic full of disease and corruption. Except our nation repent, turning from political sin to social righteousness, it cannot be saved, and will lose its divine place in the earth."

Soon Herron was much in demand around the country. At the University of Michigan he drew an audience of more than three thousand students, faculty members, and townspeople, one of the largest gatherings in the university's history. He enjoyed similar success at the Union Theological Seminary, at DePauw University, Indiana State, and Princeton. When he lectured in Montreal, a reporter compared the sensation "to the explosion of a bomb in a public square of the city." Herron told his audiences that the Christian church "was not sent to be an institutional dominion, but a sacrificial and redemptive life in the world." America's "stupid national conceit" had blinded it to "the wicked moral blindness of our industrialism."

A series of Herron's lectures was published under the title of *The Christian Society*:

> In an age which mammon rules, when property
> is protected at the expense of humanity, when

the state regards material things as more sacred
than human beings, the gospel of the kingdom
of God. . . . needs to be terribly preached as the
judgment of love to the industrial despotism. . . .
The people must finally own and distribute the
products of their own labor. . . . The condition
of competition is inconsistent with both Christianity and democracy. . . . Industrial freedom
through economic association is the only Christian realization of democracy. . . .

The nation ''was under the same obligation to sacrifice
itself for the redemption of the world that Jesus was.''
To Herron, history was, in essence, the progressive realization of the implications of Christ's sacrifice upon the
cross. ''Every commercial privilege which an American
enjoys was purchased on Golgotha. . . . The commercial
and political supremacy of the Anglo-Saxon peoples''
was ''largely due to the faith of Calvin and Cromwell in
the divine government of the world.''

Out of Herron's teaching in the 1890s came a Christian
commune in Georgia, the Christian Commonwealth Colony, and an influential magazine entitled *The Kingdom*.
The successor to *The Kingdom* was a magazine called
the *Social Forum*, which announced that ''the only true
economic and political outcome of Christianity is socialism . . . an essential part of true religion.''

* * *

Walter Rauschenbusch was the principal evangel of the
so-called Social Gospel in the early years of this century. His main theme was the responsibility of all Christians to work for social justice and, more especially, to
improve the deplorable conditions of the great majority
of working-class men and women. Jane Addams was the
exemplar of the spirit of Christian reform. Her father had
been a friend of Abraham Lincoln, who called him ''my
dear old double-d Addams.'' Addams herself planned on
a medical career but the death of her adored father in
1881 left her in a state of nervous collapse. She found
comfort in her religious faith. While she could not accept
the narrow ''late Calvinism,'' as she called the religion
of her Midwestern hometown, she returned to Cedarville,
Illinois, to become a member of the Presbyterian church
there, as the ''outward expression of religious life with
all humility and sincerity,'' and subsequently committed
her remarkable energies to the search for ''an outwarde
symbol of fellowship, some bond of peace, some blessed
spot where unity of spirit might claim right of way over
all differences.'' She found the ''blessed spot,'' or rather
founded the blessed spot, in Hull House in Chicago and
inspired several generations of young middle-class
woman to devote their lives to reforming American society.

Frances Willard, the president of the Women's Christian Temperance Union, carried the message of Christian
women wherever she went. There must be a more eq-
uitable distribution of the wealth of the nation or some

kind of revolutionary uprising would take place. When someone in her audience suggested that such talk smacked of socialism, Willard was undeterred. "If that is socialism," she replied, "so be it." Socialism or not, it was Christian justice. *The Churchman*, a Presbyterian journal, declared: "There are a thousand evidences that the present state of things is drawing to a close, and that some new development of social organization is at hand." The editor hinted that this "new development" must be some form of Christian socialism.

The New York chapter of the Christian Socialists Club met with members of the Bellamy Nationalist Club, a group advocating a form of national socialism, and in Detroit a Conference of Applied Christian Workers and Social Reformers debated how best to infuse an industrial society with the ethics of Christian socialism.

Granted the reality of Christian socialism, what was its influence on the thinking and—even more important— the behavior of the great body of Americans, Christian and non-Christians alike? I think it is clear that it worked as a yeast or leaven in the body politic. It went hand-in-hand with milder expressions of Christian reform. It was apparent in the popular literature of the day, in novels and poems. It underlay the continuing efforts to curb the grosser manifestations of capitalistic avarice. It was warp and woof of Populism, "Bryanism," and Progressivism.

Although such middle-class reformers did much to ameliorate the harsher aspects of industrial capitalism, the strongest voices of radical Protestantism were those of the farmers of the South and Midwest. Convinced that they were being cruelly exploited by Eastern capitalists and, above all, by the railroad tycoons, angry farmers began to organize for political action. The seeds of Populism lay in the farmers' organizations of the South and Midwest. They were militantly Christian and outspokenly opposed to "Wall Street." The National Grange of the Patrons of Husbandry was started in December 1867. The Grange, one of its founders wrote, "seeks to array the agricultural class, nearly one-half of our whole population, as a compact body against the evils [of capitalism]." Other organizations followed: the Farmers Alliance, the Farmers' Union, the Brothers of Freedom, the Farmers' Mutual Benefit Association, the Agricultural Wheel, and the Cooperative Union of America. The preamble to the constitution of the Texas Alliance declared that its purpose was to "secure to our people freedom from the onerous and shameful abuses that the industrial classes are now suffering at the hands of arrogant capitalists and powerful corporations." One of the most striking features of the early "alliances" and "granges" was a strong emphasis on equality between races, especially brotherhood with blacks and Indian peoples. Tom Watson's Southern Alliance called for cooperation with the Colored Farmers' National Alliance and Cooperative Union. The National Agricultural Wheel, which held its first convention in 1887 at McKenzie, Tennessee, demanded that "public land, the heritage of the people, be reserved for actual settlers only—not another acre to railroads or speculators . . . a graduated income tax,'' and ''that all means of public communication and transportation shall protect the Chicksaws and Choctaws, and other civilized tribes of the Indian Territory in all of their inalienable rights, and shall prevent railroads, and other wealthy syndicates, from over-riding the law and treaties now in existence. . . . ''

In 1889, W. Scott Morgan, who had been active in establishing the Arkansas chapter of the Agricultural Wheel, published a large volume entitled *History of the Wheel and Alliance, and the Impending Revolution.* ''The natural law of labor,'' he wrote, ''is that the laborer is entitled to all the fruits of his toil. There is no variation to this rule. It is fixed upon the universal law of nature. . . . '' In any other political system, Morgan declared, ''the selfishness of those who have unjustly . . . acquired capital . . . [by] robbing labor of its profits, would have ere this produced a revolution.'' Only a ''spirit of forbearance'' inherited from the founders of the nation had prevented such an upheaval. Nevertheless, the world was ''approaching a crisis without parallel, in some respects, in all past history.'' Anyone who doubted the imminence of such an upheaval must be ''densely ignorant'' of the ''fires of discontent'' burning in both Europe and America.

Thomas Nugent was the nominee of the People's Party for governor of Texas in 1892 and 1894. Nugent had been a district judge and was an avowed Christian socialist.

Like many other critics of "the system," he based his social criticism on the Scriptures, the works of the Founding Fathers, and on the writings of Swedish theologian Emanuel Swedenborg and American poet and essayist Ralph Waldo Emerson. In the words of one historian, "He looked upon the whole human race as being conjoined with the Lord—and this conjunction he called Divine Humanity. All things were to him a One. Each part of an organic whole whose soul God is, and whose body is man." Nugent was careful to distinguish his brand of Christian socialism from the various secular socialisms or communisms imported from Europe. In the Christian soul, he wrote, the "social brotherhood is slowly growing . . . as breast after breast thrills responsively to the sound of that 'calling.' " If human selfishness could be transcended, "glorified industries will arise in orderly unity and harmony like the 'City of God.' " The "national banking system, like Carthage, must be destroyed, and the national government must no longer be allowed to farm out its credit to corporations to be used for private gain."

An ally of Nugent and Watson was Ignatious Donnelly, a Minnesota Populist. In his best-known work, *Caesar's Column*, published in 1891, Donnelly declared that his mission was "to preach into the ears of the able and rich and powerful the great truth that the neglect of the sufferings of their fellows, indifference to the great bond of brotherhood which lies at the base of Christianity, and the blind, brutal and degrading worship of mere wealth, must—given time and pressure enough—eventuate in the overthrow of society and the destruction of civilization.'' Life ''for the great mass of mankind'' was ''a dark and wretched failure. . . . The many are plundered to enrich the few. . . . The rich, as a rule, despise the poor; and the poor are coming to hate the rich. The face of labor grows sullen; the old tender Christian love is gone; standing armies are formed on one side, and great communistic organizations on the other. . . . They wait only for the drum-beat and trumpet to summon them to armed conflict.''

In *The Golden Bottle*, another of Donnelly's political tracts disguised as a novel, the hero is a devout Christian and Kansas farmer, Ephraim Benezet, who becomes President of the United States and sets out to put the Populist platform into effect. An era of cooperation follows and the downtrodden of the world rise up against their oppressors. Underpinning all is a reawakened Christianity.

Leonard Brown, a radical Iowa farmer, spoke for hundreds of thousands of his fellow Midwesterners in his *Iowa, Promised Land of the Prophets*:

> The few grow rich, the many poor
> And tramps are dogged from every door
> The millionaire would have his word
> And e'en his very whisper heard
> And Congress bow before his nod
> And President cry ''Gould is God!''

The "kings of Capitalism" should be drowned in the Des Moines River. Then, when "grasping Greed and Avarice drown/And War and Poverty go down!"

> Love, Equality and Peace
> Shall bless for aye the human race,
> True Christianity restored,
> Mammon no longer is adored—
> All in one common brotherhood,
> The good for all the greatest good—

As Brown describes the defeat of King Gold and his sychophants, his refrain runs:

> Beware, beware
> The millionaire;
> A deadly foe, a deadly foe
> To thee, O working man, to thee.

Abandoning his verse for prose, Brown called for the establishment of cooperative farms and factories where farmers and workers would demonstrate "a willingness to be equal with our neighbor, and not above him." People must be educated "up to a higher and truer love and brotherhood. . . . Societies and lodges will be merged into the great society—the State—of which all are members, and brethren: a society of mutual helpfulness, of mutual benefits, of mutual love and good will, wherein my neighbor's child will be as dear to me as my own . . .

and every helpless creature shall have a lodgement in my heart or hearts. . . . Then will each man be indeed a very Christ of love, radiant with the spirit of the Divine Teacher.''

To make his point, Brown tells the story of two young men of equal industry. ''They go into business. The one uses as much industry as the other, and is as diligent in business, exercising as much thought and intelligence and physical power. The one makes perhaps five hundred dollars per day; the other not more than five dollars per day. Why the difference? The question is answered in one word—CAPITAL. The one is rich and has capital to invest. The other is poor and depends upon industry alone. . . . What equality is here? . . . The laws are framed to help the rich. . . . Money increases by its own growth, so to speak. . . . 'Ten per cent interest will eat the world up.' This is a great wrong.''

When the delegates of the People's Party gathered in Omaha in 1892 to draft a platform and nominate a candidate for President, the atmosphere was that of a religious revival. It recalled the euphoria of the Republican convention of 1860. The nation was in the grip of the terrible depression of that year, but hope was in the air like a tangible presence. Ignatius Donnelly had written the preamble to the most radical platform ever presented to the American electorate by a major party. ''We meet,'' it declared, ''in the midst of a nation brought to the verge of moral, political, and material ruin. Corruption dominates the ballot-box, the legislature, the Congress and touches even the ermine of the bench. The people are demoralized. . . . The newspapers are largely subsidized or muzzled; public opinion silenced; business prostrated; our homes covered with mortgages; labor impoverished and the land concentrated in the hands of capitalists. The urban workers are denied the right of organization . . . a hireling standing army, unrecognized by our laws, is established to shoot them down [a reference to the Pinkerton strike breakers]. . . . The fruits of the toil of millions are boldly stolen to build up colossal fortunes for a few, unprecedented in the history of mankind; and the possessors of these, in turn, despise the republic and endanger liberty. From the same prolific womb of government injustice we breed the two great classes of tramps and millionaires.'' Among other things the platform called for government ownership of the railroads as well as the telephone and telegraph systems.

In many states, Populists were elected to state legislatures. In some Western states, Populists won the governors' office and were elected to the U.S. Congress. A Populist with the marvelous name of Lorenzo Dow Levelling was elected governor of Kansas. Davis Waite, teacher, lawyer, union official, and devout Populist, was elected governor of Colorado. He issued a famous ''Tramp Circular,'' which he sent to all the police departments in the state, urging them to be lenient with the itinerate unemployed. ''Those who sit in the seats of power,'' he wrote, ''are bound by the highest obligation to especially regard the cause of the oppressed and helpless poor. The first duty of government is to the weak. Power becomes fiendish if it is not the protector and sure reliance of the friendless. . . . "

One of the responses to Waite's "Tramp Circular" read: "Whatever may be the opinion of the aristocrats and all the other rats, God and the people will bless you for this brave word."

So it went. The year 1893 was, if possible, more desperate than its predecessor. Henry Adams wrote to his friend, John Hay, "if I were not a pessimist and a fatalist, a populist, a communist, a socialist, and the friend of a humanist [Hay], where would I be at?" He could see nothing but "universal bankruptcy."

Despite Henry Adams's gloomy forebodings, the economy improved and Populism disappeared almost as quickly as it had appeared. The Democratic Party, with its irresistible boy orator, William Jennings Bryan, was its residuary legatee. Bryan promised, in words that echoed Martin Luther, to make "everyman a king"— and every woman, presumably, a queen—black Americans, of course, excepted. But the memory of the radical social programs proposed by the Populists lingered on. It is certainly ironic that the high tide of political radicalism in America was a tide of evangelical/fundamentalist Christians known as the Populists or People's Party.

I have alluded to the Women's Rights Movement, which traced its beginnings to the late 1848 conference at Seneca Falls, New York. Like the abolitionist movement, it too was driven by the Christian convictions of those who enlisted in it and, indeed, in the post–Civil War period, most of its leaders were veterans of the antislavery wars. The International Congress of Women, called in 1893, to celebrate the forty-fifth anniversary of the Seneca Falls Convention, was attended by delegates from Great Britain, France, Denmark, Norway, Finland, and India plus "thirty-one different associations of moral and philanthropic reforms." The convention opened with a religious service in which six women ministers participated, among them the first woman to be ordained in the United States, Antoinette Blackwell Brown. The Reverend Anna Shaw delivered the opening sermon on "The Heavenly Vision." She reminded her listeners that the woman's movement had been born out of the antislavery movement, out of women's "longing for the liberty of a portion of the race." Now God was revealing to women the world over "the still larger, grander vision of the freedom of all humankind."

There were eighty-one separate meetings during the convention, which was attended by an estimated 150,000 people.

We dare not leave the nineteenth century without some attention to another area of Christian social endeavor, specifically the American missionary women who carried the word of Christian redemption to the four corners of the globe. Work in foreign missions had a special attraction for educated middle-class women who went into the field as the wives of missionary men and as single women whose special task was to raise up native women, especially in the Middle East, Africa, and China—women who had lived for centuries under the most degrading constraints. In many countries a husband's power over his wife was absolute, as, of course, was the father's over his daughters. India held to the custom of sati, where a widow often from the upper class, was burned at her husband's pyre, and "wife-killing" was an accepted practice. Indians who would not kill a cow or a dog did not hesitate "on the slightest quarrel" to hack their wives to death. Sir Charles Napier, commander-in-chief of British Forces in India, described a scene where a seventeen-year-old girl was suspected of being unfaithful to her thirteen-year-old husband. "Her father led her to the front of his house . . . twisted her long hair in his hands, and holds her on tiptoe while her brother hacks off her head. This was all done openly," Sir Charles noted. Unwanted daughters in many Eastern societies could be killed under certain circumstances. The Ameers had their mistresses take potions to bring on miscarriages. If that did not work, "they chop up the child with a sword. . . . In Clutch they kill daughters who do not marry quickly," and in Todas, near Goa, "infant daughters were drowned in milk or trampled to death by water buffaloes and among the Belochist the girls were killed with opium."

In China, upper-class women suffered the lifelong agony of foot-binding, and concubinage was an accepted fact of life. The harem and the seraglio were part of Muslim life, and in many societies husbands were allowed as many wives and mistresses as they could support.

Loanza Benton, a missionary to Syria, was dismayed by the treatment of female children. They were not treated as well as the animals, she reported. An Arab who wished to divorce his wife simply sent her away and if she demurred, in some cases killed her.

The women missionaries founded medical clinics, schools, orphanages, hospitals, and colleges for their charges and the young native women trained in these institutions became champions of women's rights in their own countries and, often, the wives of progressive national leaders.

In 1924, a student at Mt. Holyoke College, one of the great producers of missionary women, wrote a poem about the college's missionary band:

Abigail Moore went out to India
A century ago, and Susan Waite
To China, and Fidelia Fiske embarked
For Persian cities, from South Hadley Town.
(South Hadley Town, where fertile seed was sown.)
And all across the world to desolate lands,
And lands most desolate with humanity,
They took their sisterhood, from northern ports
Up the earth's slope to sea-surrounded reefs,
Down the earth's curve to wave-embattled capes,
To Egypt and Japan and Labrador,
Hawaii, Turkey, and Colombia—
Yearly they went, not yearly to, return—
And not all to return at any time.

We talk incessantly about cultural diversity and world
unity, yet we seldom, if ever, give credit to the women
(and of course men, too) who did so much to free women
in every part of the globe from ancient burdens and injustices and in doing so helped to knit the modern world
together. In the words of one woman missionary, "The
greatest argument for Christianity was its attitude toward
women and children as over and against the attitude of
every other religion in the world toward women and little
children."

Finally, a significant form of radical protest against the
bitterly competitive character of American capitalism in
the last century was the numerous utopian communities
that sprang up so luxuriantly. Some, like Scots-born social reformer Robert Dale Owens's New Harmony colony
and Brook Farm were secular (Brook Farm was in fact
pervaded by the quasi-Christian spirit of Transcendentalism), but many more, and these the longest-lived, were
specifically Christian. The most successful, aside from
such "fortress communities" as the Shakers, Mennonites, and Dunkards, was radical reformer John Humphrey
Noyes's Oneida, or Perfectionist, community and the best
history of such ventures is Noyes's *History of American
Socialisms*. The members of these communities undertook to live the simple lives of Christian communism,
finding their inspiration in the primitive Christian communities of the first and second centuries A.D.

We have already taken note of Henry Adams's de-
spairing observation that for members of his class, Chris-

tian religion had (one is tempted to say "suddenly") lost its meaning. What had happened quite simply was that the religion of man, the religion of Reason, Science, and progress had taken hold of the imaginations of the learned class, of professors and professionals and intellectuals in general—with, of course, some notable exceptions, primarily in the ranks of Christian Socialists. Obviously this disenchantment did not affect the legions of faithful who marched under the fundamentalist/evangelical banner. They remained faithful to their Lord and Savior and to their adored leader, William Jennings Bryan. So, for the first time in the nation's history, there were two Americas—the America of the religion of man, whose stronghold was the burgeoning university with its faith in science and in Cartesian methodologies, and the "booboisie," as Henry Mencken would soon be calling them.

The symbol of the latter's marginality was the famous Scopes trial in 1925 where the brilliant skeptic, Clarence Darrow, made a fool of a confused and ailing Bryan. When Bryan died a few weeks after the end of the trial, the spirit of radical Protestant dissent died with him.

But that was not the complete story, of course. Middle-class Christian socialism and Social Gospelism, survived, finding its representative figure in a Christian minister named Norman Thomas. Thomas's quadriennel Presidential candidacies became something of a joke, but millions of Americans voted for him every four years; considerably more, indeed, than voted for his Marxist counterpart, Earl Browder. In doing so, they testified to the persistence of the city of God in an increasingly secular world. Much as the Democratic party had absorbed the Populist party, preserving, at least, the memory of its glory days, so the Democratic party of Franklin Roosevelt's New Deal took over the inheritance of the Populists, the Progressives, and the Christian Socialists.

Since Americans generally have no collective memory (that is to say, no knowledge of our history as an unfolding drama), we have no comprehension of the way in which historical episodes flow, one into another, ever widening and enlarging our sense of our humanity. We treat every great historical episode in our past as a discrete and singular event. This is a consequence in part at least of scholarly specialization so that no professor of American history knows anything of our nation's past except his own meager academic speciality.

Thus the way in which these various nineteenth-century movements reinforced and complemented each other remains one of the untold secrets of our past.

10

THE NEW DEAL

By the opening decades of the twentieth century, the city of God had a more formidable adversary than Darwinism. Karl Marx had issued his Communist Manifesto in 1848, and it had been first printed in the United States by the Claflin sisters, Victoria and Tennessee, who also headed the first local of Marx's International Union.

Between 1867 and 1894, Marx produced his *Capital*, the most systematic attack on capitalism that had yet appeared. Marx argued, as we know, that the course of history had been determined by economic factors. As he put it: "The mode of production in material life determines the general character of the social, political and spiritual processes of life." Marx borrowed from Hegel the notion of the "dialectic," involving a thesis, an antithesis, and a synthesis. Where Hegel had considered the dialectic as an intellectual or spiritual process, Marx claimed it was economic or "material," hence the classic Marxian phrase "dialectical materialism" as describing the essential nature of history. The key lay in the struggle between capital and labor. Capitalism was the most recent thesis; the resistance of the workers, the proletariat, constituted the antithesis and the classless society the final synthesis. Particularly appealing was Marx's theory of "surplus value." Capitalists sought to pay labor the lowest possible wages. The difference between the wage, ruthlessly bargained down by employers, and what the product of that labor sold for was the surplus value, the excessive profit that enabled the capitalist to live in ostentatious luxury while working men and women lived in poverty.

What made Marx's doctrines so alluring was that the conditions of labor that he described were observable everywhere that capitalism flourished.

The Marxist took seriously the Christian proposition that private property is sin. In fact, Marxists carried the proposition to its logical conclusion. Marxists said, in effect, private property is the root of all the wickedness and evil in the world. It is the means by which the innate equality of all men and women is violated. It is the means by which bitter class divisions are created, the instrument of oppression by the capitalists of the workers. If the Marxists could just do away with private property, they could create a perfect and harmonious world—the Christian millennium, in other words. It would not be too much to say that Marxism stole from Christianity two of its most basic tenets. It was able to do this because Christianity, and more especially, the Roman Catholic branch, seemed unwilling, or unable, to do anything substantial to redress the suffering imposed on the working classes by industrial capitalism. In fact, the major Protestant denominations, as well as the Roman Catholic Church, seemed all too ready to accommodate themselves to the status quo and even, on occasion, to ratify it. It thus remained for the religion of man, whose antecedents in the Enlightenment we have described, to produce an extreme wing—the Marxists.

Finally, the Marxists claimed to be "scientific." That was the magic, talismanic word. As we have seen, there had been numerous Christian "socialist" or "communist" communities since the day of the early church but they had been unscientific. Scientific Marxism would succeed where they had failed just because it was scientific. Science was not only the god of the modern world but the vector of history. Capitalism would soon be overthrown by the workers and, after a period of the dictatorship of the proletariat (required to forceably remove all vestiges of the old, class-ridden society), the repressive organs of the state would wither away and all would be peace, equality, and harmony, with each man and woman contributing according to his or her ability and receiving according to his or her needs.

It should be noted that if Marxism was the "fighting" branch of the religion of man, liberalism was the more reserved and genteel denomination, committed to discussion and debate, more at home in the library and study than on the picket line. In the religion of man, the liberal was analogous to the comfortable churchgoer who held the right opinions and voted right at the polls but who left the sacrifices and hardships of social action to the true believers, the disciples of Karl Marx.

The spectacular growth of Marxism was, above all, testimony to the cruelly exploitative aspects of industrial capitalism as well as to the perpetual dream of a peaceful and harmonious world.

Initially, Marxism, or more specifically the Communist party in the United States, had little attraction for American workers or intellectuals, but the two most far-reaching events of the first half of the twentieth century changed the political and intellectual atmosphere dramatically. First there was the Russian Revolution of 1917 and the rise to power of the Bolsheviks, led by Vladimir Lenin. The fact that one of the major nations of the world—and one of the most backward—had established a communist state suddenly gave legitimacy to a proposition that heretofore had been merely theoretical. The result was predictable: Millions of workers and middle-class reformers in various industrial nations flocked to the communist standard of hammer and sickle. The second decisive event was the stock-market crash and Great Depression of 1929. In the United States, hitherto resistant to Marxian communism, thousands joined the party and thousands more became "fellow travelers," sympathetic middle-class intellectuals and academics. What made communism especially seductive was the fact that Marx had predicted that capitalism must collapse from its internal inconsistencies and that was exactly what appeared to be happening in a worldwide depression of unprecedented severity.

Here was a religion of man that was an amplification and radical extension of the Enlightenment, French Revolution version. Not content to theorize about the nature of man and the nature of nature, it directly challenged the religion of the city of God for control not only of men's and women's mind and souls but of the social and political direction of the world. This was intellectual hardball of the most aggressive kind.

In the United States the response of the city of God was Franklin Roosevelt's New Deal. Beside the cosmic claims of Marxism, it seemed a modest response at best.

It can be seen, in fact, as a Christian socialist revolution that involved an odd alliance between Christian reformers of various stripes—Christian Socialists, Social Gospelers, Christian democrats—with Marxists, most of whom were members of the Communist Party, U.S.A. Franklin Roosevelt was himself a devout Christian. Moreover, his social reforms were directly related to his Christian convictions. Roosevelt's aide, Rexford Guy Tugwell, who spent a long life ''in search of Roosevelt,'' the title of one of his books, wrote of Roosevelt's ''deep religious faith, assumed by most contemporary commentators to be the nominal affiliation any politician would maintain. . . . The Roosevelt religion was consistent with gaiety and intellectual freedom; but it was nevertheless deeply held.'' The story was told of a young reporter who pressed Roosevelt to describe himself. Was he a communist, as his enemies alleged, a capitalist, or a socialist? What was his political philosophy? "Philosophy, philosophy," Roosevelt replied in his jesting way as though the word were unfamiliar, "I am a Christian and a Democrat."

Roosevelt's religious convictions, and his familiarity with Scripture were evident in his first inaugural. (He insisted on being sworn in on his family Bible, which was in Dutch.) His first words had a theological ring to them: "This is a day of national consecration." Of his anticapitalist fervor there can be no doubt. He made clear at once that he held the moneyed interests responsible for the economic crisis. It was they, "the rulers of the exchange of mankind's goods," who had brought on the depression "through their own stubbornness and their own incompetence. . . . They know only the rules of a generation of self-seekers. They have no vision, and where there is no vision the people perish."

As we might have anticipated, Roosevelt used the image of the money-changers driven from the temple. "We may now restore the temple to the ancient truths," he declared. Leonard Brown, author of *Iowa, the Land of the Prophets*, would have approved, as would have William Jennings Bryan. Roosevelt ended the inaugural with a final evocation of Scripture. These dark days should teach all Americans "that our true destiny is not to be ministered unto but to minister." The words were from the Gospel according to Mark. Jesus told his disciples: "Whosoever will be great among you, shall be your minister. And whosoever of you will be chiefest, shall be the servant of all. For even the Son of man came not, to be ministered unto but to minister and to give his life a ransom for many.''

Frances Perkins, recalled that Roosevelt would talk of the first inaugural in a way ''that made you realize you were on sacred ground so far as he was concerned. He would never claim credit for that. It was something not of his own making. I'm sure he thought of it as direct divine guidance.''

Rexford Guy Tugwell was convinced that one of the main reasons Roosevelt recognized the Soviet Union was that he hoped thereby to be able to exert some influence on Stalin to mitigate his campaign against religion. After meeting privately with Roosevelt to work out the terms of recognition, an astonished Maxim Litvinov told Tugwell that Roosevelt had concluded their discussion by saying: ''There is one other thing; you must tell Stalin that the antireligious policy is wrong. God will punish you Russians if you go on persecuting the Church.'' ''Does he really believe in God?'' Litinov asked. Tugwell assured him that he did.

Whether by chance or intention, a number of the people closest to Roosevelt were Christians with backgrounds in Christian social work. The most important of these, of course, was Frances Perkins, Roosevelt's Secretary of Labor and the keeper of his conscience. Frances Perkins was, like Roosevelt, a devout and practicing Christian. She had worked for Roosevelt in labor affairs when he was governor of New York. When he asked her to take

on what, given the disastrous state of labor in the Great
Depression, was the most important cabinet position, Perkins consulted her parish priest. No woman had ever held
a cabinet position, and Perkins felt misgivings about her
qualifications. Her priest told her he believed that it was
"God's own will" that she accept the job and if it was
God who had assigned her the task, "He will help you
to see it through." Frances Perkins often repeated the
story of the two charitably inclined individuals debating
why shoes should be provided for a poor man. One said,
"Because his feet are cold," the other "For Jesus' sake."
The reason for doing things "for Jesus' sake" rather than
out of a general humanitarian disposition was, according
to Perkins, that the humanitarian impulse would not last.
In the long run, it was not durable. "The poor aren't
grateful in the long run, and quarrels come up." There
was resentment over ingratitude. So kindness, compassion, and justice were, finally, "for Jesus' sake," not for
the world's. Perkins favorite passage in Scripture was
from First Corinthians: " . . . be ye therefore steadfast,
immovable, always abounding in the work of the Lord,
forasmuch as ye know that your labour is not in vain in
the Lord."

Perkins wrote that she went to Washington as Secretary
of Labor to serve her Lord, the poor and needy, and
Franklin Roosevelt. To Perkins the most basic imperative
of Christianity was "to see that the state does care about
what happens to the individual and doesn't say—'Oh,
well, it can't be helped.' " A Christian society was, by

definition, one "of social cooperation and social justice."
Perkins's closest friend in the cabinet was Henry Wallace.
Perkins and Wallace and his wife, Ilo, went to the Anglo-
Catholic Church of St. James. At the suggestion of her
priest, Perkins began visiting at least once a month a
community of Episcopal nuns in nearby Catonsville,
Maryland, for silence retreats. "I have discovered the
rule of silence is one of the most beautiful things in the
world," she wrote a friend. "It gives me time for so
many, many ideas and occupations. It also preserves me
from the temptation of the idle word, the fresh remark,
the wisecrack, the angry challenge, the hot-tempered
reaction, the argument about nothing, the foolish question, the unnecessary noise of the human clack-clack."

Henry Wallace, Roosevelt's Secretary of Agriculture,
was, like Frances Perkins, a fervent Christian. Harry
Hopkins, the aide who came to be closest to Roosevelt,
was the son of a harness maker in Sioux City, Iowa. As
a student at Grinnell College, Hopkins came under the
influence of Edward Steiner, a Czechoslavian Jew who
had converted to Christianity and who filled young Hopkins with Walter Rauschenbusch's Social Gospel of service and reform, "Applied Christianity," as he called it.
After a stint as a counselor in a Christian camp called
Christadora, Hopkins married Ethel Gross, also a student
of Steiner, who, like Steiner, had converted from Judiasm
to Christianity and began a career as a social worker.
Certainly it could not have been entirely without significance that the three members of his official family with

whom Roosevelt was in closest rapport were all committed Christians. The list did not stop there, of course. Aubrey Williams, who headed the National Youth Administration and the WPA, two of the New Deal's most important agencies, had a background as a Christian social worker and had contemplated for a time becoming a Presbyterian minister. Will Alexander, Rexford Tugwell's deputy in the Resettlement Administration, had been an active YMCA worker and president for four years of Dillard College, a largely black college in New Orleans.

Hundreds, doubtless thousands, of men and women staffing the various agencies of the New Deal were Christian Socialists or Christians of the Social Gospel persuasion who were recruited from private charitable organizations.

The other large religious group in the New Deal was, of course, the Communists, believers in the religion of man. It is one of those splendid ironies in which history abounds (and which make me eternally grateful for being an historian) that these two religions should have joined forces, often, it should be said, while harboring considerable suspicion of and even hostility toward each other. The Communists, like the Christian Socialists, labored unselfishly for the good of mankind, especially for the good of working people and the poor and oppressed. Many of them lived lives of far greater sacrifice and self-abnegation than their Christian counterparts, most of whom found positions in the New Deal bureaucracy. It is also the case that since no prospective federal employees were questioned about their political affiliations, many devout Communists found their way into New Deal agencies (State and Agriculture were especially hospitable). They served as counsels and aides to various Congressional committees, especially those concerned with labor issues, and in a variety of ways made their intelligence and dedication assets to the nation that they dreamed of turning into a replica of the Soviet Union.

Tens of thousands of Communists, who had no government employment, labored with equal, or even greater dedication ''in the world,'' defending the rights of black Americans, organizing the unemployed, stiffening the spines of union leaders, pamphleting, organizing, organizing, organizing and, most awesome of all, listening. These devout men and women, believers in the religion of man, who lived in anticipation of *the revolution*, whose faith in reason and science were touching in the extreme, listened hour after hour to the mind-numbing rhetoric of the party leaders who described in endlessly reiterated detail how the dynamics of history must before long produce the classless state.

Several simple anecdotes may illustrate the relationship between Christians and Communists. Dorothy Day was a beautiful young Marxist firebrand, a light in Greenwich Village and a friend of Eugene O'Neill. When she converted to Catholicism, she became a nonperson to her Marxist friends. In her autobiography she told poignantly of watching a Communist-led march against hunger on

Washington when her former Marxist friends passed by. "I stood on the curb and watched them," she wrote, "joy and pride in the courage of this band of men and women mounting in my heart, and with it a bitterness too that I was now a Catholic with fundamental philosophical differences. I could not be out there with them. I could write, I could protest, to arouse the conscience, but where was the Catholic leadership in the gathering of bands of men and women together, for the actual works of mercy that the comrades had always made a part of their technique in reaching out to the workers?

"How little, how puny my work had been since becoming a Catholic, I thought. How self-centered, how ingrown, how lacking in a sense of community."

Back in New York, Dorothy Day joined forces with a young friend, Peter Maurin, to set up Houses of Hospitality for the poor and hungry, for, indeed, anyone who wished to serve the Lord in poverty and humility by helping others. A year or so later, they started the *Catholic Worker*, and in time this modest beginning touched the conscience of the fat and prosperous Catholic establishment.

When the San Francisco longshoremen went on strike led by "Red" Harry Bridges, a reputed Communist, confrontation with shipping tycoons and enemies of labor erupted into bloody street fights. When the Secretary of Labor refused to recommend action to help break the strike, the rumor spread that Frances Perkins and Harry Bridges were secret lovers.

After Roosevelt had been elected President, but before he had been inaugurated, he was taking the waters at Hot Springs. To this retreat came two young Communists with a plan for saving the nation from the clutches of the Depression. The security forces toyed with calling out the National Guard but Roosevelt, hearing of their mission, said that he would be glad to talk to them. The conversation lasted several hours. When it was over, an aide expressed his admiration to Roosevelt for his kindness in listening to the youths, to which Roosevelt replied that he had found the conversation interesting. Not only was Roosevelt one of our great orators, he was, above others, Lincoln perhaps excepted, our "listening" President.

Franklin Roosevelt was not naive. He believed that the children of light should be as cunning as the children of darkness. He was well aware that the New Deal was heavily staffed with Communists but as long as they served his larger purposes he welcomed them aboard. So the Communists and the Christian Socialists, Social Gospelers, and plain old Christians worked together, the citizens of the city of God and the Marxist heretics, in one of the strangest alliances in our history.

In a deep sense, then, the New Deal was the culmination of a hundred and fifty years of Christian resistance to capitalism in the United States—and, it must be added, resistance on the part of the religion of the city of man as well. The New Deal era marks one of those moments in history when the city of man and the city of God came into a happy, if brief, conjunction. The point is high-lighted by the fact that the devotees of the most radical version of the religion of man worked side by side with the dwellers in the city of God to achieve common and fairly clear goals. The followers of the religion of the city of man did not, of course, see it that way. To them any religion but their own was an enemy and organized, in-stitutional Christianity was the greatest enemy of all. They were certainly not aware that they had borrowed their noblest ideals of equality and human unity from their Christian enemies. But facts are facts, as they say, and the facts are that this remarkable, more or less uncon-scious, and subsequently unidentified, coalition achieved the profoundest social change in our history in somewhat less than a decade.

EPILOGUE

THE SOLUTION

We began this treatise with the proposition that the end of the Cold War and the collapse of Marxism had had the unfortunate result of bestowing a kind of legitimacy on "capitalism," in part by entangling "capitalism" with "democracy" and even "Christianity." We have endeavored to expose these fallacies by following the model of St. Augustine's two cities—the city of man and the city of God—and by demonstrating that the city of God, mindful of the teachings of Christ, has persistently, if not always consistently, understood that the accumulation of wealth placed the soul of the accumulators in extreme peril. Since capitalism clearly involves such accumulations, it is just as clearly an enemy of the city of God. Since democracy is the offspring of the city of God, democracy too is, at best, in an uneasy alliance with capitalism.

Capitalism, in its simplest form, is the capacity to collect and distribute money (property) in such a way as to accomplish desired economic ends; that is to say, to make more money. This activity may or may not be to the benefit of society. In our more foolish and inattentive moments, we have simply assumed that capital activity is beneficial. Whether or not we subscribe to such jejeune notions as the famous trickle-down theory, or its ill-favored twin, supply-side economics, we are disposed to believe that capital activity is in itself "good," is, in fact, particularly if not uniquely American. It is to this frame of mind, of course, that we owe the junk-bond scandals and, most dramatic of all, the savings and loan fraud. Capitalists own and operate the runaway industries that rob American workers of decent jobs and hustle off to Korea or Indonesia to exploit the working people of those countries. Capitalism, under the banner of free speech, has capitalized sex and turned pornography into a multibillion-dollar industry, to the shame of the nation.

Capitalism is of course pleased to borrow from democracy the freedom, or liberty, of free enterprise and the "free market" or, in the nineteenth-century term, "laissez-faire—to allow to do things freely." It is also delighted to turn the ordinary democrat into a consumer and fatten off of him or her. But capitalism, by the same token, inevitably seeks to exploit or abuse the freedom that it is so ready to borrow and the victim is the democracy itself, which is abused and perverted.

The notion that capitalism and democracy—and even Christianity—have some essential connection has been reinforced by the fact that Christianity and Marxism demonized each other. Indeed, it was often claimed that the Cold War was simply a struggle between the legions of the Lord under the banner of "capitalism" and the armies of Satan with the *Communist Manifesto* nailed to their standard. It became evident that many right-wing Christian fundamentalists were far more interested in destroying the Satanic Soviet Union root and branch in a final bloody Armageddon than in trying to reach some accommodation with the persecuted and oppressed peoples of the Soviet Union and the Soviet Bloc. In their hearts many of them, I fear, wanted a war of extermination, not peace and reconciliation.

The collapse of international Communism (some Marxists, I suppose, will still argue that Marxism had yet to be given a fair trial, dismissing the Soviet Union and its bloc as a perversion of "true" Marxism) demonstrates a number of historical truths, perhaps the principal one of which is that you cannot use the coercive powers of the state to force people to "be good." You can certainly use it, hopefully with restraint, to keep people from being "bad," although even this is not clear in our present age. That is to say you cannot force people, except for relatively brief periods, to eschew the ownership of property, for example. Yet private property remains a sin in the eyes of the residents of the city of God and a constant source of social disequilibrium in the city of man.

If we needed to be reminded, as theologian Reinhold Niebuhr tried to remind American Marxists in the 1930s, that power corrupts, the history not simply of the Soviet Union but every one of its satellites should remind us of that imperishable fact, as true a law as history affords.

That is to say, the collapse of the Soviet Union reminds us of the doctrine of original sin. What, in the last analysis, brought Marxism down was the simple, ancient fact of original sin. To impose any political and/or economic and social system on a people requires the use of arbitrary force, or power, in one form or another, and *the greater the power, the greater the corruption*, a fact the city of God has known since its beginning—and which, it must be confessed, it has often ignored. The Founding Fathers knew, of course, and so did our old friend, William Manning, the farmer of dubious literacy.

The collapse of Marxism also reminds us that God's greatest gift is the gift of His freedom, the freedom that gave a handful of English settlers in colonial America who experienced it in their faithful communities the courage to change the world—the inspiration for what Wyndham Lewis called "radical universalism." The history of the Communist bloc countries reminds us that without freedom the noblest ideal becomes as dust.

One of the distinguishing features of Marxism was its impatience. It could not bear the thought that the millennium might be centuries away. The Marxists wished to force history by violence. By the same token its demise should remind us that it takes at least three generations of devoted effort to achieve any significant reform. It took some three generations from the days of John Woolman, one of the early Quaker opponents of slavery, before the slaves were freed, and another three or four generations before black Americans began to receive the most basic rights of Americans. It was the same with the campaign for the rights of women. From the Seneca Falls convention of 1848 when Elizabeth Cady Stanton called for the vote for women. The fact is that the religion of man is lacking in stamina. As we have seen, it expects immediate results and has little capacity for dealing with the tragedy, suffering, and defeat that are such common aspects of human history. The city of God, on the other hand, kept alive the hope of equality and democracy for two thousand years in the face of endless setbacks and disappointments.

There are doubtless other lessons to be learned. I trust that one of them is the hollowness of the pretensions of Reason and Science to rule the world. Or the notion that we can develop something called the ''social sciences'' that will inform us about the true nature of men and women; or that we can rely on psychology to, in effect, replace religion. The fact is that since the last decades of the nineteenth century, psychology has made precisely that claim.

If Marxism is, or was, the most potent, and recent, form of the religion of man, liberalism has always been its weaker, or more discreet, sister, or ''denomination.''

Liberalism, although it has been understandably reluctant to face up to the fact, has suffered severe, if not irreparable, damage in the collapse of Marxism. Liberalism shared many of the ideals of Marxism even if it deplored its methods. Like Marxism, it believes in Reason, Science, and progress and is hostile to religion in any form, except the religion of man. From its stronghold in the universities, it has dominated American intellectual life since the beginning of this century—almost a hundred years!

If we need confirmation of the unhappy state of liberalism, we need look no further than the reflections of a scholar generally regarded as the most eloquent spokesman of that battered creed. Richard Rorty, professor of humanities at the University of Virginia, in a recent article describes the attitude of the ''contemporary American liberal to the unending hopelessness and misery of the lives of young blacks in American cities. Do we say that these people must be helped because they are our fellow human beings? We may but it is much more persuasive, morally as well as politically, to describe them as our fellow *Americans*—to insist that it is outrageous that an *American* should live without hope.'' The point that Rorty wishes to make is ''that our sense of solidarity is strongest when those with whom solidarity is expressed are thought of as 'one of us,' where 'us' means something smaller and more local than the human race.'' To Rorty that is why sympathy extended to a person simply because he or she is ''a human being,'' is ''a weak, unconvincing explanation of a generous action.'' This attitude seems to me a bizarre retreat from the dream of the unity of humankind in the direction of that tribalism that is the curse of this era.

It must be said for Marxism that it held fast to just that

human solidarity that Rorty so casually abandons as "weak [and] unconvincing."

Rorty presses his argument. "It is," he writes, "part of the Christian idea of moral perfection to treat everyone, even the guards at Auschwitz or in the Gulag, as a fellow sinner. For Christians, sanctity is not achieved as long as an obligation is felt more strongly to one child of God than to another. . . ."

A fatal weakness in Rorty's argument is that the solidarity with "fellow Americans" on which he found the liberal ethic, would never in a thousand years have provided the human energy to free the slaves because clearly slaves were not "fellow Americans." They were, instead, far more profoundly fellow "human beings," God's children, *equal in the eyes of the Lord if not equal in the eyes of the great majority of white Americans*, more than equal, most precious in the eyes of the Lord because most suffering and oppressed.

For Rorty, it is one of the weaknesses of "secular ethical universalism" that it "has taken over this attitude from Christianity." Quite the opposite is the case. It has indeed taken over "ethical universalism" from Christianity and therein lies its greatest strength, *but* in divorcing itself from the larger Christian system, it left itself vulnerable to the distortions characteristic of the religion of man—impatience, poverty of the affective life, arbitrariness (believing it knew better what was good for the poor and oppressed than they knew themselves), and a barrenness of spirit.

The fact is a Christian cannot but be pleased that the city of man has adopted the principal articles of the Christian's "social faith"—democratic equality for all people—multiculturalism, if you will—and, beyond that, faith in the unity of mankind. That dwellers in the city of man may be, and indeed usually are, quite ignorant of the origin of these tenets of Christianity is far less important than the fact that they have become norms for the enlightened "seculars," and with, it might be said, the addition of "environmentalism" come to constitute the central elements of *their* religion. Rorty is thus somewhat in an odd spot, in that while understanding the source of liberalism's "secular ethical universalism," he nonetheless rejects it in favor of tribal "solidarity."

We are witnessing in our colleges and universities the consequences of Rorty's notion of "solidarity" with "one of us." "One of us" turns out to be, typically, the smallest possible "human unit"—Asian Americans, Native Americans, Hispanics (or Latinos, or Chicanos), and subdivisions of subdivisions: gay Asian Americans, gay African Americans, and so on. One woman announced to a friend of mine recently that she was withdrawing from her support group because she only felt comfortable with other Jewish lesbians. Is this the solidarity that Rorty has in mind?

If the religion of the city of man is in tatters, what of the religion of the city of God? Certainly on the face of it it does not seem very promising. The fundamentalist/evangelical wing of Protestantism has not only abandoned its nineteenth-century tradition of radical dissent, it has allied itself with the reactionary political right-wing and saddled itself with the antiabortion crusade. To deplore abortion, to be deeply opposed to abortion, those are perfectly legitimate positions, but to seek to impose their own convictions on everyone else *by law*, to criminalize what is a traumatic enough experience is foolish, undemocratic, and, I fear, un-Christian.

So as things stand now we can obviously expect no help from that quarter, which is disheartening in the extreme because, among the deluded, are many decent and devout men and women who should be employed in a better cause. As for the ''main-line'' denominations, they have become, for the most part, spiritual comfort stations for the middle class.

The city of God is, of course, neither Roman Catholic nor Protestant. It is the city of all faithful Christians of whatever division or denomination. If the story of Protestant Christianity has been the most dramatic and significant story since the sixteenth century, we should bear in mind that for some fifteen hundred years the Roman Church held the world together. It preserved through tumultuous and desperate times the dogma, doctrine, vision, and the dream of the unity of mankind. It elevated the status of women through the cult of the Virgin, through nuns as the brides of Christ, through the ideal of chivalric love to a status far higher than that accorded women in any other of the great religions of the world. The vast hierarchy of the Church, however corrupt it became in the end, worked for a thousand years to keep scholarship and learning alive, and, in a hundred specific and identifiable ways, to lay the foundations for the modern world. It must be kept in mind also that the first Reformers—John Wyclif, Martin Luther, Jan Hus, and hundreds of others—were themselves priests trained in the teachings of the Roman Church and determined to restore it to health.

The Reformation produced the Counter-Reformation and much bitter and bloody fighting, but the Roman Church was itself reformed in the process and if it, initially, allied itself with monarchy and reaction, against all the clamorous divisions of Protestantism, it reasserted itself as the Church Universal. Today, with almost a billion of the faithful scattered in every corner of the globe acknowledging the pope as their pontiff and spiritual leader, the Church is in an ideal position to bear powerful witness to the city of God. In the countries of Latin America, the zealous reforming priests and nuns fight now on the side of the desperately poor and dispossessed, and Latin Catholicism promises much in the endless fight for social justice.

It may indeed be the case that the Protestant sects and denominations whose fragmentation has been one of the scandals of Christendom are now to take a backseat. Certainly there seems to be little enough energy and true piety in the American Protestant churches, the black churches excepted. So let us consider for a moment the black churches of America.

I still recall how startled I was to read in an essay of

Arnold Toynbee's some fifty years ago the statement that the hope of Christianity in the United States rested with the black churches. Toynbee's observation has often come back to me over the years. I think its truth is indeed self-evident. From emancipation in 1863 on the black churches have expressed "the souls of black folk," as in the title of W. E. B. Du Bois's famous book. Black ministers have been the *spiritual and political* leaders of their congregations. The city of man that they perforce lived in is the city of the *white* man. The city that they have lived in and in which they make continually "a joyful noise to the Lord" is the city of God, and black Christianity is the only fully developed form of democratic Christianity because the black congregations *respond*. This one fact, which whites are inclined to view patronizingly, gives black Christianity its remarkable vitality. Myles Horton, the founder of the Highlander Folk School in Tennessee, told of the anxiety and confusion experienced by the young Martin Luther King, Jr., in the early days of the Montgomery bus strike. When King expressed his fear and uncertainty to Horton, Horton told him, "Martin, take it to the people," by which he meant "Go to your congregation and ask them to tell you what to do." The congregation held up King's hands and gave him the courage to organize and maintain the boycott.

In black Christianity, the two cities come closer to merging than in any other sphere of American life, whereas white Christianity, as we have noted, is full of disappointments. Can the black church revitalize the city of God? Stranger things have certainly happened in the long history of Christianity. One has only to recall that there are more Christians in black Africa than in white America to be reminded of the universal reach of the Church and of how small a part of that vast reach the United States in fact is.

The announced purpose of this exercise has been to disentangle democracy and Christianity from capitalism. Why? In order to free Christianity, if, indeed, it wishes to be freed, to assume its classic role as the critic of capitalism. Since it is my conviction, and that, I suspect, of a good many other men and women, that there must be something beyond capitalism, something better than capitalism, at least as we now know it, and since Marxism, which claimed to be it and which quite obviously isn't, is defunct, *how are we to think about the future?* It is my conviction that the way in which the city of God in centuries past thought about the future brought about the most positive aspects of our present-day world: the ideals of equality and democracy, the hope of world unity, and the brotherhood and sisterhood of men and women.

We live in a secular world, which is as it should be or at least as it must be. It seems safe then to assume that the city of man, striving for justice and, above all, for peace, and the city of God, hopefully true to its faith till the end of time, are going to go on coexisting, sometimes cooperating and sometimes at odds, as far into the future as the mind can reach.

INDEX

Abbott, Lyman, 153–54
Abolitionist literature, 146
Abolitionists, 140–48
Adams, Charles Francis, Jr., 150, 152
Adams, Henry, 149–50, 152, 167, 171
Adams, John, 116, 125, 126, 129–30, 133, 137, 138
Adams, John Quincy, 111
Addams, Jane, 158
Address to the German Nobility (Luther), 45
Aeneid (Virgil), 126
Alexander, Will, 184
All Souls' Day, 27, 110
Ambrose, Saint, 17
American Revolution, 126–30
Anthony, Susan B., 137
Antin, Mary, 1

Aristotle, 35, 50–51, 100
Augustine, Saint, 17–24, 34, 47, 99, 110, 189

B

Bacon, Francis, 102
Baptists, 78
Baxter, Richard, 85–87, 92–93
Becker, Carl, 102, 105, 127
Bel Inconnu (Renart), 31
Benedictines, 26
Benton, Loanza, 170
Bible, 9–16, 40–41, 52–53
Bible, books of
    Daniel, 78
    Deuteronomy, 10
    Ecclesiastes, 11–12
    Exodus, 9

Bible (*cont.*)
  Genesis, 12–13
  Isaiah, 12
  Job, 11
  Leviticus, 9, 10
  Luke, 13, 15
  Mark, 13, 14, 15, 17, 180–81
      Matthew, 15
  Proverbs, 10, 11
  Psalms, 10, 11
  1 Samuel, 10–11
Bible Commonwealth, 65, 69,
      84–85
Bill of Rights (Revolution
      Settlement), 83–84
Bill of Rights (Virginia),
      110–11
Black Americans
  and Christianity, 199–200
  racism, 147–48, 167
  slavery, 122–24, 138, 140–
      48, 153, 193
Bora, Catherine von, 51–52
Boston Chronicle, 121
Bradford, William, 63–64
Braintree covenant, 67–68
Bridges, "Red" Harry, 186
Brook Farm, 171
Browder, Earl, 172
Brown, Leonard, 163–65, 180
Brownson, Orestes, 140–42

Bryan, William Jennings,
      167, 172
Bryant, William Cullen, 146
Bunyan, John, 87–88
Busch, Moritz, 136
Bushnell, Horace, 154–55
Butler, Frederick, 127

C

Caesar's Column (Donnelly),
      162
Calvin, John, 53–59, 61, 89,
      110, 157
Capital (Marx), 175
Catholic Worker, 186
Catholicism. *See* Papacy
Celibacy, 28–29, 42, 50
Channing, William Ellery,
      139–40
Chapman, John Jay, 152–53
Charles I, 75–76, 77, 83
Charles II, 81, 82–83
Christian Church (Eastern),
      17, 33
Christian Church (Western),
      16–17, 25–27
Christian communes, 157
Christian communism, 78–79,
      171, 177
Christian Directory . . .
      (Baxter), 86

Christian Humanism, 33–35, 37

"Christian Liberty" (Luther), 48–49

Christian reformers, 137–39

Christian socialism, 139–40, 149–73, 161–62, 173, 177, 179, 184

Christian Society, The (Herron), 156–57

Christian Union and Progress, Society for, 140

Christianity
  and capitalism, 2, 3–4, 7, 49, 69–70, 78–79, 85–93, 189–91
  and celibacy, 28–29, 42, 50
  and democracy, 2–3, 27, 66, 132–36
  and equality, 7, 111, 128–30
  Greek influence on, 33–35, 100–01
  and poverty, 9–16, 38–39, 40–41, 42
  and revolution, 81–82
  women, status of, 27–31

Churchman, The, 159

Cicero, 23, 24

Cistercians, 26

City of God, The (Augustine), 17, 18–24, 66, 110

Claflin, Tennessee, 175

Claflin, Victoria, 175

Cluny, monastery of, 26–27

Communism
  and Christianity, 42, 78–79, 175–77
  collapse of, 3, 189, 191–94, 200
  and the New Deal, 184–87

Communist Manifesto, 175, 191

Community of Mankind, 79

Community of the Earth, 79

Complete History of the United States . . . (Butler), 127

Concerning the Married Life (Luther), 52

Constance, Council of, 42, 43

Constantine the Great, 16

Convents, establishment of, 29–31

Copernican system, 115

Covenants, 67

Crates the Theban, 57

Croly, Herbert, 1

Cromwell, Oliver, 76–78, 81, 157

Cromwell, Richard, 81

D

Dana, Richard Henry, 143–44

Darrow, Clarence, 172

Darwin, Charles, 150

Darwinism, 3, 147–48, 150–52, 175

Day, Dorothy, 185–86

Declaration of Independence, 109–10

and property, 110–11, 119–20

Democracy

and capitalism, 2, 6, 190–91

and Christianity, 2–3, 27, 66, 132–36

as a guiding principle, 7

and property, 110–11, 119–20, 124–25, 140–41

and Puritan townships, 68

stability of, 112, 117–18

Democracy in America (Tocqueville), 132, 134

Descartes, René, 95–101, 102, 106, 153

Diggers, 79–80, 110

Discourse on Method (Descartes), 96, 97–98, 101

Donnelly, Ignatious, 162–63, 165

Du Bois, W. E. B., 199

Dunkards, 171

Dutch Reformed Church, 61

E

Eliot, Sir John, 75–76

Emerson, Ralph Waldo, 162

Encyclopedia of World History, 26

End of History, The, 2

England, Church of, 59, 61, 62–63

reform of, 65–66

England, Commonwealth of, 77–81

English Civil War, 73–82

Enlightenment, the, 3, 95–107, 109–10, 179

Episcopalians, 114

Equality as a guiding principle, 7, 111

Eusebius, 17

F

Farmers' organizations, 160–61

Federal Constitution, 109, 112–22, 124–25

and slavery, 122–24

Federalist Papers, 120

Fifth Monarchy, 78

French Revolution, 104–05, 125, 128–30, 179
Friedell, Egon, 106

G
Galileo, 100, 101–02
Gladden, Washington, 154
Golden Bottle, The (Donnelly), 163
Great Depression, 178–79
Great Protestation, 73–74
Great Rebellion, 73–82
Greek cultural influence
  on Christianity, 33–35, 100–01, 104
  on the Federal Constitution, 112–14
Grimké, Angelina, 144
Gross, Ethel, 183

H
Hamilton, Alexander, 117–18
Hammer and Pen (socialist magazine), 154
Hay, John, 167
Heavenly City of The Eighteenth Century Philosophers, The (Becker), 102, 127
Heer, Friedrich, 31
Hegel, Georg W., 175

Heretics, burning of, 42, 43
Herrick, George, 58
Herron, George, 155–56
History of American Socialisms (Noyes), 171
History of the Plymouth Plantation (Bradford), 63–64
History of the Wheel and Alliance, and the Impending Revolution (Morgan), 161
Honorius, Emperor, 18
Hopkins, Harry, 183
Horton, Myles, 199
Hume, David, 104, 106–07
Hus, Jan, 43–44, 51, 52, 89, 198
Hussites, 59
Hutchinson, Anne, 69
Hyde, Edward, 77

I
Independents, 59, 78
Individualism, 90–92
Indulgences, sale of, 43, 44
Institutes of the Christian Religion (Calvin), 54, 58, 61
Interregnum, 73–82
Iowa, Promised Land of the

Iowa (*cont.*)
    Prophets (Brown), 163–
    64, 180

J
James, Saint, letters of, 15
James I, 73, 75
James II, 83
Jay, William, 143
Jefferson, Thomas, 110–11,
    125, 129, 138
Jeffreys, Judge, 86
Jerome (Bohemian monk), 43
Jerome, Saint, 17
Jesus Christ, 13–14, 28, 39,
    56, 180–81
John of Gaunt, 41
Justin, Saint, 18

K
King, Martin Luther, Jr., 199

L
"Laboring Classes, The"
    (Brownson), 140–41
Lenin, Vladimir, 178
Leo, Pope
Levellers, 80, 110
Levelling, Lorenzo Dow, 166
Lewis, Wyndham, 126, 192

Liberalism, 193–95
Lincoln, Abraham, 158
Lilburne, John, 79–80
Litvinov, Maxim, 181
Lollards, 42, 78
Longfellow, Henry
    Wadsworth, 146
Lowell, James Russell, 146
Louis XIV, 83
Luther, Martin, 41, 44–49,
    50–53, 58, 89, 100, 110,
    167, 198
Lutheranism, 59

M
Madison, James, 120–21, 125
Manning, William, 121–22
Martin V, Pope, 33, 42
Marcellinus, 18
Marx, Karl, 175
Marxism, 3, 4, 175–77, 191–
    94, 200
Mary, the Virgin, 30
Mary Magdalene, 28
Mason, George, 110–11, 123
Massasoit (Wampanoag
    chief), 64
Maurer, Heinrich, 93
Maurin, Peter, 186
Mayflower Compact, 62

Mencken, H. L., 172
Mennonites, 171
Mercantilism, 70–71
Methodists, 88–89
Micah, 67
Mill, John Stuart, 150
Missionary movement, 168–71
Model of Christian Charity, A (Winthrop), 66–67, 84
Monastic orders
  and agriculture, 26
  development of, 26–27
Montesquieu, Charles-Louis Joseph de, 114
Morgan, W. Scott, 161
Morris, Gouverneur, 119–20, 124
Moses, 29
Milan, Edict of, 16

N
Napier, Sir Charles, 169
Natural law, 115
New Deal, 173, 179–88
New Harmony colony, 171
New Model Army, 77, 80
New Views of Christianity, Society and the Church (Brownson), 140

Newton, Sir Isaac, 115
Niebuhr, Reinhold, 191
Noyes, John Humphrey, 171
Nugent, Thomas, 161–62

O
Oneida (or Perfectionist) community, 171
Owens, Robert Dale, 171

P
Papacy
  corruption of, 33, 37
  excommunication of, 48
  indulgences, sale of, 43, 44
  and Martin Luther, 44–49
  Pope as Antichrist, 39–40, 90
Parker, Rev. Theodore, 142–43
Paul, Saint, 15, 28–29
Peasant uprising (England), 41
Peirce, Charles Sanders, 151–52
People's Party platform, 165–66
Percy, Lord, 39
Perkins, Frances, 181–83, 186

Peter, Saint, 15
Philosophers
    French, 104–06
    and nature, 103–04
Pilgrim's Progress (Bunyan),
    87–88
Pilgrims, 61–64
Pinckney, Charles, 116–17,
    123–24
Plato, 34, 35
Populism, 159–67, 173
Potter, Henry Codman, 154
Predestination as Protestant
    doctrine, 37–38
Presbyterians, 59, 78
Present, The (religious
    magazine), 140
Principles of Psychology
    (Spencer), 150–51
Progressives, 173
Protestant ethic, the, 4
Protestant Ethic and the Spirit
    of Capitalism (Weber), 3
Protestantism
    and capitalism, 49, 69–70
    and congregation, 69
    predestination & free will,
        37–38
    radical, 131–48
Puritanism

and capitalism, 5, 69, 85–
    93, 131
and democracy, 68
and theocracy, 85
Puritans, 64–69, 73–82

R
Ramsay, David, 127
Ranke, Leopold von, 6
Rauschenbusch, Walter, 158,
    183
Reason, Age of, 95–107
Reformation
    divisions among, 59
    English, 37–42, 53–59, 61,
        62–63, 90–92, 198
    German, 41, 44–53, 198
Religious Union of
    Associationists, 140
Renart, Jean, 31
Republic (Plato) 34
Restoration (England), 81, 82
Revolution Settlement, 83–84
Robespierre, Maximilien,
    127–28
Roman Empire, collapse of,
    18–19, 25
Roosevelt, Franklin D., 173,
    179–81, 184, 187
Rorty, Richard, 194–96

Rosenstock-Huessy, Eugene, 27

Roundheads. *See* Puritans

Russian Revolution, 178

S

St. Peter's Basilica, 44

Samoset (Wampanoag Indian), 64

Scopes trial, 172

Shakers, 171

Social Darwinism, 150

Social determinants, 7

Social Gospel, 158–59, 183

Solomon, 11

Sophia, Queen (Czech), 43

Spencer, Herbert, 150–51

Squanto (Wampanoag Indian), 64

Stalin, Joseph, 181

Stanton, Elizabeth Cady, 193

"Stanzas on Freedom" (Lowell), 146

Steiner, Edward, 183

Straw, Jack, 41

Sudbury, Archbishop, 41

Swedenborg, Emanuel, 162

T

Tawney, R. H., 59

Temperance movement, 137–38

Tertullian, 18

Thacher, Rev. Samuel, 126

Theses (Luther), 44, 51

Thomas, Norman, 172

Tocqueville, Alexis de, 132–36

Toynbee, Arnold, 199

"Tramp Circular" (Waite), 166–67

Transcendentalism, 142, 171

Trevelyan, George, 82

Trialogus (Wyclif), 43

Twelve Conclusions (Lollards), 42

Two Years Before the Mast (Dana), 143

Tyler, Wat, 41

Tugwell, Rexford Guy, 179, 181

U

Universal History . . . (Ramsay), 127

Utopian communities, 171

Utopianism, 2

V

Virgil, 126

Volusian, 18

W

Waite, Davis, 166–67

Wallace, Henry, 183

Ward, Lester, 151

Washington, George, 111

Watch-Word to the City of London, A . . . (Winstanley), 80

Watson, Tom, 160, 162

Weber, Max, 3–4, 5, 17, 49, 85, 87, 88, 89, 91, 131, 149

Wenceslaus IV, Emperor, 43

Wesley, John, 70, 88–89, 124

White, Andrew, 152

Whittier, John Greenleaf, 145

Willard, Frances, 145, 158–59

William and Mary, 83

Williams, Aubrey, 184

Winstanley, Gerrard, 78–80

Winthrop, John, 66–67, 84

Wolfe, Don, 79

Women
convents, 29–31
missionary movement, 168–71
and Puritanism, 68–69
status of, 27–31
violence against, 169–70

Women's Christian Temperance Union, 158

Women's Rights Movement, 167–68, 193

Woolman, John, 192–93

World unity, 7

Wyclif, John, 29, 37–43, 51, 52, 78, 86, 89, 110, 111

Z

Zwingli, Huldreich, 89

ABOUT THE AUTHOR

Page Smith was born in Baltimore, Maryland, in 1917 and attended the Gilman School. He received his undergraduate degree in English from Dartmouth College, where he studied under the influence of the late Eugen Rosenstock-Huessy. Smith was named a Rufus Choate Scholar, and after graduating from Dartmouth, he spent five years in the United States Army, where he served with a Tenth Mountain Division. When the war ended Smith decided to do graduate study in history under the GI Bill. He attended Harvard University, where his dissertation director was Samuel Eliot Morison. He received his Ph.D. in 1951.

In 1962 Smith's biography of *John Adams* was published. Five years in the making, this two-volume biography received Doubleday's Kenneth Roberts Memorial Award, Columbia University's Bancroft Award in American History, and a nomination for the National Book Award. It was also a popular Book-of-the-Month Club Main Selection. Smith is also the author of *A People's History of the United States*, an eight-volume, six-thousand-page work. Seven of the volumes were also Book-of-the-Month Club Main Selections. His most recent book is *Killing the Spirit*, a critique, in historical perspective, of the current crisis in American higher education. Smith was the founding Provost of Cowell College, the first college at the University of California at Santa Cruz, and he is currently associate director of the William James Association.